The Miners

At rest in peace, released from misery
Are those who laid the basis of our industry
Men, women and infants of tender years
In darkness shared their lives in toil and fear
From their tortured bodies flowed the wealth of kings
From the indominitable spirit a cry of justice rings
The playing fields of Eton never felt their measured gait
A life of virtual serfdom was their fate
No inglorious carnage had their conscience to atone
The lives which were lost were but their own
No role of honour bears their humble names
Creating the nations wealth was the irrefutable claim
Their memorials are inscribed in sweat and blood
Upon seams of coal and putrid mud
Their blood still courses vigorously through veins
Of those descended of that mining strain
In a subterranean world amidst incessant conflict
They cement the bonds of loyalty and comradeship

Dick Tank, Betteshanger miner from 1945

Sixty Years of Struggle

History of Betteshanger Colliery

By Di Parkin

Published by Betteshanger Social Welfare Scheme

Edited and Designed by Andrew Williams

All photographs provided by CHIK at Dover Museum

Published by Betteshanger Social Welfare Scheme.
Magness House Mill Hill Deal Kent CT 14

Printed by Kingfisher, Wills Road, Industrial Estate Totnes TQ9 5XN

ISBN - 13 978-0-9557550-0-2

Grant aided by Kent County Council and Awards for All National Lottery

Front Cover photo: Men coming up after the 1960 stay down strike.
Rear Cover photo: Early Betteshanger colliers in front of Headgear.

CONTENTS

Di Parkin and John Moyle delivered versions of chapters 4 and 5 to the Ruskin Public History Seminar and the London Socialist Historians Group.

INTRODUCTION

Betteshanger colliery a militant pit

'Betteshanger' literally means, a 'steep wooded slope by a building'. It looks back to the Old English 'hangra', a 'wood on a steep slope', combined with 'bytle', a 'house or building'. It is first recorded in 1176, as Betleshangre. "(Kent Place Names)

There is no wood now, no coal mined now, on the windy hilltop not far from the sea in East Kent.

The name Betteshanger sounds Saxon and old, yet it means most as a place of sharp, full pitched class struggles. From the 1930s, through the war, 'stay down' and national strikes, to the pit closure in 1989.

It is for those events that Betteshanger will be remembered; this book is part of that remembering.

The Coalfield Heritage Initiative Kent (CHIK) has, in its community archive at Dover Museum, constructed a history of some aspects of the Kent coalfield. However, the CHIK project in assembling the history of the Kent field:

> "Made a conscious decision at the outset not to concentrate on the industrial disputes - feeling that this area had already been to some degree over emphasised." (CHIK, 2006)

Far from it, there is no complete history of the class struggle at the Kent pits, in particular there is no history of this the most militant of pits, Betteshanger.

As a recent commentator on the CHIK website remarks on the heritage.

> "It is pleasing to see that there are some people out there who wish to remember the Coal Industry in Kent and the people who worked in it. I worked in Chislet, Tilmanstone and Betteshanger collieries and I find it hard to see how the industry has been removed from the map without any acknowledgement of heritage." (Ex-miner writing on the CHIK web site, 26th September 2006)

It was in order to acknowledge and celebrate that heritage that Betteshanger Social Welfare Scheme (BSWS) sought and was awarded a small lottery grant and a further grant from Kent County Council, in 2006, to write this book.

Author's interest

It was in 1972 that I first met Betteshanger miners on the picket line at Dover docks. This was during the national strike over wages and conditions. A number of students from Canterbury went to join the picket against the unloading of scab coal. There were pictures in the national press of a student friend being menaced with an iron bar.

After the strike was over, we went weekly to the Betteshanger pit. We stood by the bus stop selling the Socialist Worker, or delivering door to door in the Circle for the regulars. This is where I first met Peter Holden. Another of my roles was as driver for the students from Canterbury in the summer of 1972.

The miners clattered down off the bus or, dark eyed, trudged up towards us, after the shift, as we stood in nervous awe with our papers. Behind us, under the big office windows, was the canteen where large women in big aprons served chips, mushy peas and pies. Some times my small son came with me. He thought, 'The Mines' was a place where you were allowed to eat chips.

"They'd come in off the bus, get the check, get their chewing tobacco and go in the canteen for a pie. They was the best things they did in there, they was like bricks!

Then they'd go round the corner, go and get in their pit clothes, grease their boots to try to stop the wet getting in, they'd get their lamps and stand there outside having a last fag." (John Moyle, 2006)

That was the beginning, in 1972, for Betteshanger and me; meeting Peter Holden, John Moyle, Barney Wynn, Brian Foy, Jack Young and others and going to meetings in the Miners Welfare at Cowdray Square. By 1974 I lived in Oxford, went to the picket line at Didcot power station and later met Betteshanger miners when they came to courses at Ruskin College. We met again on the picket lines at Grunwick's in North London, a bitter strike for union recognition.

Losing touch with the individuals in the 1980s, as a PhD student studying the social history of the Second World War, I went back to 1942 and wrote a chapter on wartime strikes. This included Betteshanger. It wouldn't go away for me: Betteshanger; It was always there, brave, militant and heroic.

I became reacquainted with Betteshanger and its miners during the 1984/5 strike. Living in Hackney, I worked at the Greater London Council's Women's Support Unit and supported Women Against Pit Closures, marching with them on a long hot day in the summer of 1984. During that summer John Moyle, on strike duties in London, came to stay at our house in Hackney and had his tape recorder and brief case stolen from his car further down the street. In 1986 we visited him and his family in Deal, but managed to loose touch again.

In 2004, Betteshanger came to me again, in the twentieth year celebration of the start of the 1984 strike, where Arthur Scargill and John Moyle spoke.

It was after that meeting, during a time when I was engaged in work on equal opportunities in Kent, that we decided to apply for a grant and write this history.

Methods

This is a celebration of the lives and struggles of the Betteshanger miners and their families. A struggle which officialdom wishes to forget. So the main voices that need to be heard are the voices of the mining community itself. Across the generations right up to the age of 90, we interviewed 27 past miners, their wives, sons, daughters and friends. Those victimised, pushed down, battled and who overcame. It is these voices which hold centre stage in this account. I was also pleased to speak with Arthur Scargill on the subject.

The voices of miners and reports of their struggles are found in the newspaper reports of the day, the Deal, Walmer, Sandwich and East Kent Mercury. Their voices can be heard in the mid 1970's oral history conducted by my friend Gina Harkell and in the records of Albert Newton (transcribed by his daughter Josephine Dempster). He had a hut storing bikes and selling cigarettes at Betteshanger in the late 1920s and early 30s.

Importantly, we studied the views and actions of the Betteshanger Branch of the Kent Mineworkers Association (KMWA) and examined the minute books of the National Union of Mineworkers (NUM), still held in Magness House in Mill Hill. Furthermore, the area records of the union were studied; these were transferred to the Kent Archive at Whitfield Dover, they included minute books, correspondence, posters and collection sheets relating to various disputes. And finally, from the Public Records Office in Kew, the official records of the State were explored, including those of the Ministry of Labour, the Ministry of Mines and the Ministry of Fuel and Power.

We looked at the work of other historians including the official historian

Page Arnot, Malcolm Pitt's work, 'The World on Our Backs' and 'Once a miner', (Snowdown, Kent) republished by CHIK. Other resources used included the report on the Wilberforce Enquiry, plus a number of theses and works on the Kent pits, housed at the University of Kent, such as those of Johnson and Goffee. A Deal History Society report, by Rutherford, on the coming of the miners to Kent was reviewed. And, both the CHIK Archives Project (voices and photos) and the Mass Observation Archive, at the University of Sussex, proved invaluable.

Throughout the project, I have benefited from constant dialogue with Betteshanger Social Welfare Scheme trustees and a number of ex-miners. I thank Sheila Shooter for providing tea and encouragement at Magness House. It should be noted that men from other Kent pits also contributed similarly to the efforts in the struggle described here, men such as Jack Collins and others.

This book is dedicated to all the men who died in pit accidents, or through dust choked lungs, in the service of the 'black stuff' at Betteshanger. Dedicated too, to the lives ruined by closure and victimisation together with their families, who struggled alongside them.

As Mrs Grant, from one of those families, said:

"I am proud to be of mining stock."

So should all those with a connection to Betteshanger, be deservedly proud, as I am to have met you.

Di Parkin 2007.

Di Parkin lives with her husband in South Devon; she works, battling injustice, as a consultant on Equal Opportunities. She has three children and four grandchildren.

SIXTY YEARS OF STRUGGLE

THE ARRIVAL OF THE MILITANT MINERS IN KENT IN THE 1930s

1

The Kent coalfield opened in the 1920s, with the Betteshanger pit coaling in 1928.

> "They was trampin, trampin, down here from Durham, Scotland, every mining village you could mention in Britain." (Mr McEwan in Harkell, 1978)

They were drawn to the area because of the expansion of the coalfield. The company Pearson, Dorman and Long (PDL), the owners of Betteshanger, had combined in 1921 with the intention of creating a great coal, iron and steel industry in Kent. (Goffee Thesis, 1978)

The original incentive to come to Kent was undoubtedly the prospect of full-time work in a new coalfield with higher than average wages. Unemployment in the traditional mining areas was as high as 50 per cent, sometimes even higher, so a constant stream of miners and their families left the dole queues of the north of England and South Wales to come to the 'Garden of England'. The Kent Coalfield was the last to be developed in Britain. Between 1925 and 1935 output in the four pits of Snowdon, Tilmanstone, Chislet and Betteshanger rose sharply, running counter to the general trend in the industry. The Kent pits were closer to the markets of southeast England and because they undercut their competitors, the demand for coal in Kent was constant. The labour force increased from a total of 2,044 in 1925 to 7,409 in 1935; over 5,000 more miners, with and without families.

Gina Harkell, an oral Historian interviewed 35 miners and their families in 1973. Her interviewee Mr McEwan sets the scene:

> "Before the miners arrived, roving teams of sinkers, like the navvies

before them, who had built the railways, sank the pits.

There had been unemployment in the mining areas all through the 1920s and not only young miners, but also family men were seeking work. They had homes of their own but no work, and were looking for places to which they could bring their wives and children. Then came the 1926 General Strike, followed by a long lockout of miners, and at the same time the colliery was getting into full production and men were needed. Hearing of the openings in Kent, men made their way – some by bicycle or on foot if they had not cash for the fare. They were shabby and ill equipped after months without wages and they took what rooms they could get and worked hard, very hard, saving for a home if one could be had. North Deal people, themselves not too well off in work or pay, were willing to let rooms but critical of their tenants – their poor clothing, their overcrowding and different ways of speech." (Mr McEwan in Harkell, 1978)

But not all the sinkers were from outside the area. In 2006 we interviewed a certain Charles Grant, a Deal man. Born in Deal, he was a Marine until 1926. He bought a small shop there but sadly the business went bankrupt. He then applied for a job with PDL as sinker at Betteshanger. It was to take two and a half years to sink the pit.

"They started sinking the 2,300 feet shaft, 22 feet in diameter. They almost had to abandon the colliery because of the green sand (which let water in). A German firm came over and put a freezing agent to keep the water back and that's still there today. When we went down on top of the cage you could feel water hit you like pinpricks where the freezing agent had rotted away." (Charles Grant, 2006)

At the pithead the workers lived in twelve "sinkers huts". Provided by PDL these huts were a simple wooden and tin affair.

"There was no electricity, no facilities. But we had a choir, football team, a band and played pitch and toss with coins. Then they built the houses in the circle at Betteshanger – the ones in the middle circle were bigger, they were for officials." (Charles Grant, 2006)

A local man, who delivered paraffin at the pit in the 1920s, remembers:

> "At Betteshanger, in 1926 they had sunk the shaft and there were two to three sheds there – no pit had baths. The miners would come out all in their black and that was a terrifying sight to a 16 year old. "

Miners came down to Deal from the North, from Yorkshire, from every mining part of Britain.

> "Miners in Kent had accents from every part of the country." (Janet Dunn, 2006)

Early Headgear at Betteshanger

Deal people gave the miners some aggravation.

> "At the time I started at the pit I suppose there was as many sinkers as there were colliers. Now the sinker was a drifter, he was a rough hand, and I remember the first Saturday night I was in Deal I saw two of them stripped off to the waist fighting bare fist in the churchyard in the High Street. Now just imagine the impression, it would make on a seaside town in Kent, that kind of episode, and so that all miners were of the same category - the sinker type." (Billy Marshall in Harkell, 1978)

With their father already in Deal, Dennis Bent came down from Nottingham on the back of a lorry with his mother, brothers and sisters.

"We had no furniture, nothing." (Dennis Bent, 2006)

"A lot of miners walked to Kent; some of them even washed in the sea on their way." (Cynthia White, miner's daughter, 2006)

"We came when I was 13, from Rotherham; I used to pick coal on the tip up there, so mum could bake bread. Then Dad came on his bike to Betteshanger and queued up to get a job; he hadn't had anything to eat and drink." (Sheila Shooter, 2006)

Goffee points out that the men came to Kent pits from every coalfield in Britain and that miners coming to Kent after the 1926 strike and lockout were likely to be extremely poor.

Albert Welford, interviewed in 2006, came to Betteshanger in 1926. A deputy, Mr Sylvester, from the Leeds area, had come up and signed him on. He left Yorkshire because although they were technically on a six-day week they would get laid off after they had wound a certain tonnage. They might work for three days and be three days on the dole. This was something that didn't happen at Betteshanger.

"We all got on together. Miners all get on with each other. It took a little while to get used to the different ways of working, about 6 months or so. We had miners from all over, we even had a black man; we had Bevan boys. Miners worked terribly hard, they'd have heart attacks and have to go back to work and they'd have hernias so big you could see them." (Albert Welford, 2006)

When Albert Welford started, the manager was Kiers, with his son as under manager. After them came a man called Mottershead.

Jack Dunn, former worker at Betteshanger, later Branch Chairman then Kent area Secretary of the NUM, described the hardships in a video interview with Hywell Francis. He met thousands of miners, particularly from South Wales, who were malnourished after the strikes in the 1920s who were walking to Kent. They were not fit to work and would collapse before they had even done a day's work.

"We had Scots, Durham, Lancs., Staffs, Derbyshire miners. It was like a cocktail, they all had a different dialect, and all gave a different name to the same tool. They had different habits and cultures, so it was difficult to get a quick coalescence." (Jack Dunn in video interview with Hywell Francis, South Wales Miners Library)

Others recorded these early days. Albert Newton, later a local businessman, kept records of his experiences at the pit, transcribed by his daughter Josephine Dempster. He began by selling cigarettes at the pithead. Later, in 1932, he had a lease from Lord Northbourne for two sheds outside the colliery gates with a rent of £25.00 per annum. Charles Grant remembered Mr Newton's shed and Jones' shop.

"Mr Newton, he built a shed, you paid 6d a week for him to keep an eye on bikes. Jone's shop was open morning, noon and night. You'd ask Mr Jones for a cup of tea and a fag. 'One and one'" (Charles Grant, 2006)

Mr Newton's notes of his observations and conversations with miners in the late 20s and early 30s tell the story of one man who walked all the way from Wales.

"One chap walked all the way from Merthyr Tydfil: Gerry Quick. It took him a month to walk. In 1926 feeling the pinch when the strike ended, he had heard of the Kent coalfield and decided to try his luck. He walked to Gloucester; it took him a week. He got a ride on an old banger, walked and got lifts. He swept streets in Newbury for a while. He then got on a goods train to Croydon, going north rather than south and east by mistake, he rode in an empty wagon. He did fieldwork and he would knock on doors and say 'I am not a beggar, I am an out of work miner' He cut out a cardboard box and made inner soles for his shoes from it. He had not washed for a month by the time he arrived; he was hungry after 4 months of (1926) strike and one month of vagrancy. He hobbled up to the pit yard:
'Are you a miner?' they asked
They called another Welshman 'Taffy' to give him a hand.
'Look at the poor buggar's feet!'

'Take him to Mrs Jones and get him something to eat'.
Taffy and his mates acted like gentlemen towards Gerry. Everybody
wanted to take him home to stay at their house! He was kept for 2
weeks and did not pay 1d such was the hospitality. After 4 days rest
he then showed up got a lamp and started work". (Albert Newton
in Dempster, transcribed in 2006)

So people walked or cycled like Arnold Moyle and his father, making
their way to Betteshanger and the other Kent pits.

A local historian explains where they were housed:

"Messrs Pearson, Dorman and Long had already built at Betteshanger
itself, housing for their necessary safety men and deputies, without
whom the pit could not function – so they were settled in Circular
Road and Broad Lane near where they were needed. During the worst
of the housing shortage, there had been plenty of demonstration of
the needs, including that of Councillor Bill Marshall, who paraded
the streets in a woman's dress and pushing a pram, with a placard,
'Miners wife and baby but no house' He was the first miner to be
elected to Deal Borough Council. Deal people were unwilling to
take miners as tenants for their houses (there were still some to let

Betteshanger began to take shape in the late 1920s

6

in those days) and discriminating advertisements 'No miners need apply' were too common." (Barbara Rutherford, 1976)

Billy Marshall confirmed this in the 1970s:

"There was no pithead baths and we used to come into Deal and spread over the town to our various lodgings in our pit clothes and our pit dirt. I don't know if I told you the story of the two old ladies who had a holiday down in Deal and when they got back they were asked how they'd enjoyed themselves, what did they think of Deal, and they said they'd enjoyed themselves immensely, quite enjoyable, but they said 'Do you know, we've never seen so many chimney sweeps in our life!" (Billy Marshall in Harkell, 1978)

"They seemed to regard miners as some kind of weirdoes - a man who can go and grovel in the earth, he must be lacking. He doesn't deserve any sympathy and they despised us." (Mr Sumner in Harkell, 1978)

Mrs Grant, a miners' daughter, said, "My family are thoroughbred miners, I am proud to be a miner's daughter." She went on to say:

"We all lived in Northbourne. We were all treated terrible; no one would speak to us. In the shops there were bacon pieces 'fit for miners'. We came from another mining area; from a house with a flush toilet to a toilet we had to empty. We couldn't a get colliery house. We asked Lord Northbourne for a house and he asked what kind of house do you want? We said with a flush toilet and bath. He said why do working people want that? We said for the same reasons as you would!" (Mrs Grant, 2006)

When the miners began seriously house hunting, real animosity was aroused.

"Deal was late and slow with its Council house building – Alderman Dobson had had difficulty in persuading the Council to recognise the need, and the few just built, Allenby Avenue, and Mill Road Terrace, were not enough for Deal's own needs and miners were not likely to come high on the housing lists. At the same time, remembering the 'sinkers' and their no doubt often unacceptable habits." (Barbara Rutherford, 1976)

This animosity is described in a letter to a local paper (*below*).

Billy Marshall described the impact of miner's migration on the town of Deal, where many Betteshanger miners and families lived.

"As the big houses on the seafront were giving up the ghost as the result of the depression in bed and breakfast, they were being occupied by miners who let out rooms and there was perhaps three or four families to one of these big houses on the seafront. We were treated as something apart. We were alien, completely alien to them. I remember coming out of

Young and McGrath.

DEAL REFUSES TO BUILD HOUSES FOR BETTESHANGER.

On Tuesday evening the Deal Town Council had before them a proposal from Messrs. Pearson and Dorman Long to build houses for the miners at Betteshanger. The proposal was that the whole of the finances should be provided by Deal and the houses taken over on a forty years hire purchase lease by the Company—100 houses in the first instance and 400 to 500 later were spoken of. The Ministry of Health suggested 50 in the first instance, and then the Company suggested that Deal should form a Public Utility Society, and the Ministry agreed. There was a long debate, one councillor calling it an iniquitous proposition, the Company having received £2,000,000 under the Trade Facilities Act why should they come to a little town like Deal to finance them. Another councillor said that they did not want this class of resident. Ultimately the recommendation to agree to the Company's proposition was defeated by nine votes to six.

Dover Express. 13th July 193

Council meeting having failed one day to get anything out of them about- the housing there, and I was almost in tears and the' padre, the chaplain for the Council, I went to him and I said, 'What's wrong, why can't we make any progress here?' 'Well', he said, 'you know Councillor Marshall, I can understand it to some extent,' he says, 'they've now moved into Swans Road and that used to be one of our best roads." (Marshal in Harkell, 1978)

But later houses were more plentiful and an attraction to some miners' families moving from elsewhere.

"We went in two rooms at Mongeham at first, until they built the houses up here; there was no roads at first, but you could have your pick of houses." (Sheila Shooter, miner's daughter, 2006)

"My husband (who had been blacklisted in Fife coalfield) said, 'What about going to Kent. Oh, you are guaranteed a house.' So that was bliss, hot water and an indoor bathroom, we had never had that before." (Mary Fowler, miner's widow, 2006)

People were happier when they got to Mill Hill.

"It was all miners very close and friendly. Grandmother got a house straight away because there were three men working" (Mrs White, miners' daughter, 2006)

"The miners wives looked after each other; the lady next door was from Yorkshire and she knocked on the door when I arrived and said, "I've left sticks and coal and set a fire and there is bread and milk" (Mary Fowler, Miners' widow, 2006)

Why was Betteshanger militant?

Miners came to Betteshanger only after the General Strike, whereas many had begun to come to the other Kent pits before the strike. Many of the miners arriving in Kent after 1926 had been black listed in their old areas for militancy.

"In the 20s and 30s the bosses had a whip hand and they came down heavily on the wages and conditions of miners." (Henriques and Slaughter in 'Coal is our Life', 1956)

In this book miners in Yorkshire explain that after the 1926 defeat, coal production did not decrease, men were sacked and conditions worsened. This bequeathed 'a legacy of bitterness among the men, who for so long had to work in conditions where their comfort was the last consideration'.

SIXTY YEARS OF STRUGGLE

These were the kinds of men who came to Kent.

Goffee's informants, working at Snowdown reported, 'being pushed around' in the area they came from.

> "They took down this file, the black book – they'd say. 'No work for you here'. All around Bolton area and there was no checking up in Kent." (Goffee, 1978)

Many miners we interviewed gave the same account, of not having work after the 1926 strike or being too militant, like Sheila Shooter's father.

> "He couldn't get a job in the Fife coalfield because he had been blacklisted for refusing to work when he was owed 12/6d for a shift." (Mary Fowler, 2006)

> "The story goes that after working an extra shift he was not paid the going rate. An argument ensued, resulting in dad being blacklisted form the entire Fife coalfield." (Mary Fowler's daughter Sylvia Watson, 2006)

> "I opened my mouth too often. (so was black listed)"
> (Albert Welford, 2006)

Albert Newton gives the same account.

> "Within this crowd of new men at Betteshanger were not only good miners who had lost their jobs, but also the no-good mischief makers, chronic absenteers, Union action stirrers and Communists ready to disrupt the normal working life of the pit." (Albert Newton in Dempster, 2006)

According to Jack Dunn the explanation for the pits' militancy lay in many factors.

> "In Kent a number of factors came together. In Betteshanger, (the pit I loved) we followed the best Welsh Tradition; we had a library in

the miner's club and 15/16 people used it regularly every day, they'd come in and read Hansard, follow the debates on the industry. There were some who had come to Kent under assumed names as they had been blacklisted in their area. (and a few who's come with changed names leaving their wives behind!)" (Jack Dunn, video, South Wales Miners' Library, Swansea)

One of the other explanations of the greater militancy of the pit was its long wall working which favoured solidarity. This is where men worked in fairly large teams along a long coalface.

The system of working varied between collieries. Miners at Tilmanstone and Snowdown worked in smaller groups in 'Room and Pillar' or 'Pillar and Stall' mining, where men worked coaling in pairs or threes in a small area, the size of a small room or stall where you might keep a horse. This is while Betteshanger colliers worked as a larger team.

"In Betteshanger you used to work as a team along the wall – twenty men. In Betteshanger, if one man was falling behind they'd send another to help him out, and I seemed to like that teamwork better than this cut throat businesses." (Mr Sumner in Harkell, 1978)

All this created a working mix. There were existing militants, a system of team working and a strong union branch. As part of the later tradition of political education, there was a library, something promoted strongly by Jack Dunn together with tutors Professor D'Eye and John Thirkell.

From the traditional mining heartlands in Scotland, the north and Wales, people looking for work desperately marched south. Many of them, leaving their home coalfields after the 1926 strike and lock out, were particularly militant and unable to get work in their own areas. They arrived to find a place where men stood up for better conditions than they left and workers' education was valued. In the testimonies of eye-witnesses and scholars alike, Betteshanger started to emerge as a vibrant and diverse new life for miners and their families.

The start of the union

Jack Dunn remembered how hard it was when he started in 1930 at Snowdown with only 300 members of the Mine Workers Federation (MWF). Others describe the difficulties:

> "When I left Tilmanstone and came to Betteshanger, Betteshanger was the weakest pit I'd ever known. We had a manager there named Mottershead, and to my way of thinking he was nothing more or less than a Fascist. He used to come strutting across that pit yard, and there was always men queued up for jobs, and he used to wave them away – he seemed to enjoy it. He was thoroughly detested. He used to walk about the pit and didn't half show his authority. You got the sack for the least thing because he knew that there was always people waiting to take your job and of course you needed a lot of guts to stand up to him and of course this had a bearing on the weakness of the Union." (Mr Sumner in Harkell, 1978)

At Betteshanger a Union Box was put up next to Mr Newton's shed in 1928.

> "It was agreed in July that 4 men would stand at the colliery gates to persuade fellow workmen to join the Betteshanger branch of the Kent Mineworkers Association." (KMWA minutes, 1928)

> "George Marsh Branch Secretary had another hut next to Mr Newton collecting for Union subs. George Marsh: 'thoroughly antagonised management.'" (Mr Newton in Dempster, transcribed in 2006)

The Union box was then also used as a Doctor's Surgery, thereby paid for by the Union. A telephone was put in and shared between medical and Trade Union business. There was also a Doctor's Committee and a Doctor's Scheme run by the Union.

In the early days the KMWA Betteshanger Branch Committee discussed issues such as the Recreation Ground, the Bowling Green, the lighting of roads 'from the Union Office to Pritchard Piggaries'. They also campaigned for pithead baths and that these should not be paid for by Union funds. By 1931 the Pit Head baths were in place.

Reading the Branch Minutes (now housed at Magness House in Mill Hill Deal) gives a clear impression of the militancy of the day.

From its early days the Branch held the view that it was a class struggle. The Branch Committee complained about disparaging remarks made about miners at the Council Housing Committee and condemned the attitude of a past General Secretary of Miners Federation of Great Britain (MFGB) for criticising another official.

> "To an audience of Capitalists. It is his duty to criticise inside the movement, but not to be used as an instrument by our opponents. He needs to set an example to his humbler comrades." (Branch Minutes, late 1920s)

In late 1928, the Branch objected to the 'employment underground' of men who had no previous experience of coal mining, counter to the coal miners' recruitment act. There were objections too about 'the officiousness' of the deputy, Mr Sylvester. Later there was a delegation to protest about the way he treated his workmen. This issue later came to a head in strikes in the 1930s, described in the next chapter.

The branch conducted a ballot on the Butty System. This was the system where one man took on and paid miners, almost as sub contractors. He would then keep much of the money on the docket (pay slip) for himself.

All union members pledged to get their comrades in the Union. At the beginning of 1931 they held a pit gate meeting to discuss putting forward a 14-day notice to abolish non-Unionism, something the Snowdown pit had already agreed.

SIXTY YEARS OF STRUGGLE

At the beginning of 1932, it was agreed to put 'notes on the lamps of non-Unionists'. The identified non-Unionists who were dismissed were then not allowed to join the Kent Mineworkers Association (KMWA).

By February 1933 Trade Union Membership was a condition of employment. At Betteshanger, 1,781 were employed underground at that time.

In August 1932 they were discussing with the National General Secretary the manager Mr Kyle's 'attitude to the committee' which was described as disparaging.

Other complaints cited that colliery officials were instructing men to work through their snap time (their meal time). It was recommended 'that we deal in stern measures with this question'.

They protested again about class collaboration.

> "That this Branch, having considered the Delegate's Report on the MFGB Conference repudiates the class Collaboration Policy of the Federation and recognising the inevitability of struggle calls upon the KMWA to immediately prepare the necessary machinery to carry out a successful struggle at the end of 12 months and in the meantime an intense campaign be wage to prepare the minds of the men for that Instruction to the Executive – moved by W Marshall."
> (General Meeting Betteshanger Social Club, 5th June 1932)

Conclusion

Men came to Betteshanger after the deprivation of the General Strike. Many of them were already militants, or at least determined to shake off the worst practices of their past coalfields. They bonded together as a working class community within a hostile area, developing workers' leadership, education and information. The union was a strong vehicle for getting pit head baths, abolishing the butty system, obtaining decent housing and resisting bullying by management. A tradition of militancy

14

was formed by the early 1930s and carried forward in later disputes, strengthening that tradition as it went.

SIXTY YEARS OF STRUGGLE

STRIKES OF THE 1930s

2

On May Day 1936 the local paper reported that thousands of miners marched 'as usual' through Dover, where they held a rally. The Betteshanger Branch was there carrying its new banner, reading: "Educate, Agitate and Organise."

Billy Powell was the Chair of the Kent Mineworkers Association (KMWA) and John Elks was it's Agent, or Secretary as it's called today. John Elks, a full time employee of the local union, addressed the crowd. He announced:

> "...they came from Wales, Scotland, Lancashire and Yorkshire and they should work for the principles for which they stood in the Kent coalfield... helping do things better than they found them in the coalfield from which they came." James Griffiths MP for Llanelli added, "When there was a disaster the public wept for them, and when there was a strike the public cursed them."

The branch was always internationalist. A resolution passed in 1936 stated: 'The only hope of the workers was the establishment of Socialism...'

They expressed their admiration of the progress made by the workers of the Soviet Union and condemned Italy's aggression against Abyssinia. They expressed their, '...firm conviction in complete unity of the working class and the return of Socialist Government with measures such as Pensions at 55, five day working for 6 days pay.'

This commitment to the working class and determination to better the conditions from their pits of origin, resistance to bullying and attacks on wages, led to many strikes.

The Ministry of Labour records at the National Archive contain large ledgers, usually one a year, with handwritten records of all disputes in all industries. The details were wide-ranging. For mining the records identify the pit, the occupations of mine workers, the number of firms involved, the date the dispute began and ended, the number of working people involved, working days lost, causes and results of disputes.

In November 1936 an important Betteshanger dispute is recorded: 'Dispute arising out of complaints by boys as to the attitude of two Deputies.'

The dispute initially lasted three days and the record stated, 'Work resumed pending an enquiry'.

However, four days later they record another strike from the 25th November to the 3rd December because of, 'alleged failure of management to carry out the terms of the agreement reached as a result of earlier dispute'.

The result of the dispute was, 'Work resumed pending an enquiry'.

Newspaper reports speak of miners getting 'relief payments' at this time.

The Government official subsequently decided that, 'the deputies in question should not be employed in an official capacity involving the change and control of men and/or boys until after the lapse of 9 months'.

In November 1936 there was another long strike. It was reported in the Deal, Walmer, Sandwich & East Kent Mercury, November 1936:

"BETTESHANGER COLLIERY DISPUTE : *Over 3,000 men idle*
PIT BOYS AND 'TYRANNICAL' DEPUTIES

Over 3,000 men employed at Betteshanger Collier are idle and the pit is at a complete standstill. The management still refuse to accede to the men's demands but state that the pit is open to men if they wish to return. It is understood that 35 summonses are to be issued against the men and boys for breach of contract.

In an interview with a 'Mercury' reporter this (Friday) morning. Councillor G Daughtrey of Deal, Secretary of the Betteshanger Branch of the Kent Mine Worker's Association said 'At a meeting at Mill Hill on Thursday night, we refused to return to work until the two Deputies complained of, are removed'. Every one of us was adamant on that. Previously, however, Mr W Kyle, the General Manager, had told the miner's representatives that the colliery company would prosecute every man for Breach of Contract. If that is so, the cases will come up at Wingham Petty Sessions. It has been stated today that only 35 of the men will be summoned, as representing the other men, but I know nothing of that. I do not know how long the strike will last, whether for three days, three months or three years. There was a meeting of the Executive at the Dover Headquarters on Wednesday morning, but up to the present I do not know if any of the other collieries, or all of them are coming out. There is a possibility that they might.'

The stoppage is the outcome of steadily growing dissatisfaction with existing conditions at the pit, which came to a head on Tuesday morning when two pit boys complained of an alleged 'tyrannical attitude' of two Deputies. As the boys refused to return to their work they were ordered from the pit, others struck in sympathy, and they were followed by the whole of the men, the absence of the boys, who are largely responsible for the haulage of the coal from the pit face to the surface, causing a complete disorganisation of the work of the pit.

In the afternoon, the conference between the management and representatives of the Kent Mineworkers' Association, ended in a deadlock, a request by the boys that the two deputies should be removed being refused. A large number of the men held a meeting in the evening at the Mill Hill Welfare Institute and decided to support the boys on the grounds that the deputies 'were not suitable persons to be in charge of the boys, and that until they were removed from their official status there would be no work at the colliery.'

On Wednesday, the Union Officials tried to persuade the men to return to work, but without success, and even the pit bath attendants stopped work in sympathy with the boys' demand. In addition to the miners and boys the engineering staff was also idle, and the next move of the management was awaited."(Mercury, November 1936)

As a means of discipline in the pre-war period, coal companies took miners individually to Civil Court to collect damages for Breach of Contract. The tariff of fines was agreed between the Mine Workers Federation (MWF) and the coal owners. But by 28th November 1936 it was reported that the summonses taken out against 35 strikers by PDL had been withdrawn.

The East Kent Mercury reported on 11th January 1937, 'The Kent Colliery owners offered an increase of 5d a shift (boys 2½d)'. In the same edition the Deal Education Committee is reported as discussing preparations for feeding school children in the event of a coal strike: 'They did not want trouble in the town. If a strike came and they were not ready, there would be trouble… they needed to provide food for miners' children if the occasion arose.'

The enquiry into the 1936 dispute, presided over by Mr. W Cook, Mines Department, was held in Deal Town Hall. Kyle and Mottershead appeared for the management, with Elks and George Daughtrey for the Union. Mr Cook said that, 'in all his years mining an inquiry on these issues was unique.'

Terry Harrison (Betteshanger NUM branch secretary in the 70s and 80s) explained:

"It was a big stoppage; it lasted 6/8 weeks and culminated in a public enquiry at Deal town hall chaired by Cook from the ministry of mines. People like Jock Elks and George Daughtrey were putting the case, which was defended by Kyle and Mottershead. There were two officials: Yates and Sylvester who had been perceived as bullying and chastising these boys. At the end of the enquiry, it found in

Soup Kitchen in 1938

favour of the union. Cook said that he didn't want to take anyone's livelihood away and listening to the union, they didn't want to see Yates and Sylvester dismissed. Cook gave them a rubbing down and them removed from having anything to do with young people." (Terry Harrison, 2006)

Thus this strike set the tone for Betteshanger. Although there was action over wages, from the 1930s to 1984 the significant strikes at the pit were over bullying and redundancies.

The long 1938 Strike

In the Ministry of Labour Records, the numbers of days, that "work people" are off work, are documented.

An example of an entry for Betteshanger records:

> "1938, dispute lasting less than a day, respecting conditions in relation to a wages settlement – made between 'firm and work people's Trade Union' and 'against the engagement of a trammer,

following work people's refusal to perform tramming without time and a half'."

For the uninitiated, a trammer is someone who pushes along tubs of coal underground, while keeping them on the rails.

In another strike, only involving the night shift, the 'lamp of a boy was stopped'. If management did not want someone to go down the pit, they would remove their safety lamp from it's hook in the lamp room. This was because the boy had failed to report, as ordered, to a Manager.

In the spring of that year there was the long dispute of May and June.

"Work people's demand that employees recently suspended owing to closing of part of the colliery should be reinstated on ballot system." (Ministry of Labour, 1938)

There had been an earlier closure, as a result of industrial action, and Management wanted to pick and choose whom it took back, rather than allowing the Union a say. This would mean that militants would not be taken back.

According to Wilf Aldred, interviewed in 2006, the 1938 Strike was also caused by a deputy Joe Yates swearing at one of the haulage boys, although poor wages were also an issue. The strike had an unusual aspect, with miners handing themselves into the workhouses.

"We'd been on strike for several weeks and we got the men together in Mill Hill and marched down to the Labour Exchange at Park Street in the town. It was packed with miners – we were after some money, some relief.

There were about 1,600; we filled Park Street with miners, so they dispatched us, because we were demanding relief – money.

This Chief Inspector of Police called out:

'I want all the A's and D's here' so I was an A and 'gathered round';

there was two coaches drew up, the next thing we know was we was off to the workhouse! We didn't know where we were going, but it was to Minster to the workhouse, it's demolished now. So off we went to it, I was 16 and we had a really good time there! The guys in there, the vagrants, had to work, they were gardening, making benches, we used to go down there with them and they made us walking sticks!

We were more or less guests there; this guy came along, a warder, and said: 'You boys you've got to work.' We said we came to get away from work, we're on strike! One of us, a German lad, threw a bucket down the hall at the warder, saying we are not going to work, we're miners on strike!

All the miners were dispatched to workhouses all over the country, Chatham, Gillingham. We were the lucky ones, we were the nearest at Minster, so we decided to walk home, I think it was June, it was lovely. So we walked home and got our bikes and went back there. We drove the warder mad; we used to go riding round all the cherry orchards and fruit orchards. We even went down to Birchington singing with a cap, to get money to go out in the evening. Arnold Moyle, he came back to get his best shirt to go dancing.
We must have been reinstated, ...we went back after. Yates was moved away not to deal with boys, it was a victory." (Wilf Aldred, 2006)

Further research on this dispute revealed a sudden jump in the usual occupations of workhouse inhabitants. Public Assistance Records (workhouse records) at Maidstone Archive show that for Dover, in June 1938, the previously listed gardeners, baker boys, OAPs, scholars, etc., came to include many more miners among their ranks.

On 5th June there were two names listed: Luke Feeny and Henry Sugden – miners. By 12th June there were three more names: Walter Dickens, William Egan & Fred Pinkney - miners. On 15th June more join them, including Arnold Moyle. Five days later John Arnold Moyle, grandfather of the present John Moyle, joined them. There is also a record of Bill

Iverson, Jack Sheavills and Harry Peat. The numbers admitted in early June amount to 40 out of the 86 total 'inmates'. Six days later they were all discharged 'at their own request'.

The admission book for the Eastry workhouse shows a similar picture of 76 admitted, including Wilf and Fred Aldred. Wilf seems to have been admitted twice on the same day, perhaps this is because he had to come back again on his bike! Here too are John Moyle's other grandfather and an uncle Harold Kirk.

Another register of 'inmates' lists everybody in an alphabetic index book. In this register we notice something strange, in two cases only wives came to the workhouse too. Ethel Allen of Cavell Square, Deal, next of kin is given as 'miner John Allen, in this institution'. She was admitted on 16th June 1938 and not discharged, it would appear, until 30th July. Her husband John, on the other hand, was admitted on 18th June and discharged with the other miners on 26th June, over a month earlier.

There was another surprise; there was a whole family in the workhouse. James Wood of Circular Road Betteshanger, with his wife and children. They all seemed to have been there for two days.

Why was a whole family there on one hand, and on the other, in the main, just individuals? Why were so few wives with their husbands? It may be possible to speculate that the admission into the workhouse was more a political act than a necessity.

In this register are the records of the next of kin and where they lived. There are miners whose links are still in County Durham or Staffordshire. Others give their next of kin as a friend. For example, Robert Curry cites John Sheavills.

There were letters in the local paper about the strike, the local Labour Party Parliamentary Candidate complained about 'dictatorial management' and another countered: 'Let us shake these extremist (militants) off.'

On 4th June 1938, The East Kent Mercury reported other Unions, such as NUPE (National Union of Public Employees) supported the strike.

The paper also reports that miners, Reg Burgess and George Tazey, were prosecuted and bound over for taking coal from the tip during the strike.

Conclusion

Both these significant long disputes in the late 1930s concerned bullying, the treatment of boys and not just wages. So miners at Betteshanger have had a tradition of taking a stand on wider issues, rather than just their bread and butter. In the next chapter we will look at the bread and butter, as well as the day-to-day 'rag ups' and disputes which took place throughout the comparatively short life of the pit.

SIXTY YEARS OF STRUGGLE

NORMAL LIFE, WALKOUTS AND RAG-UPS 3

From all the material, it is clear that the pattern of day-to-day industrial relations remained fairly similar throughout the 1930s and 1950s, as well as at other times. An account will be made of how 'rag ups' (walkouts) and disputes occurred and why they happened. We describe a way of going on that existed in the 1930s through to the 1980s.

It is important also, to remember that, "Miners want to get coal" (John Moyle, 2006) and that at other times they would be engaged in the very hard graft of production.

How things were organised

It is important to understand the system at work in the pit. On each face there would be someone, (like a charge hand in other industries), who was known as the Puffler (he had a deputy called the Monkey Puffler). The men chose this person as their representative. He was the one who got the docket each week which explained what people had earned and he would be the one to take up with the management, any disputes about the docket and the contents of the pay packet. The Overman would measure the amount of coal and that would go on the docket. There were different teams with given numbers such as '90s' or '104s'. The miners 'on contract' were in regular teams, as were rippers, face work colliers or pan turners. Extra men were 'on the market' to be allocated where necessary.

Many of the disputes were about payment, about not paying the correct allowances for things like working in water, waiting time, or problems with materials. These would often lead to 'walk outs' or 'rag ups'

Protest gathering at Betteshanger

Various people we interviewed comment on the incidents when people left the pit:

"The worst period for walking out was 1930s, was when the Barnsley men came down, the conditions were terrible until 1948. The conditions were bad everywhere, perhaps you'd be working in water and they wouldn't pay you water money. So you'd walk out; there was a lot of water in Betteshanger." (Dennis Bent, 2006)

Jack Dunn's widow, Janet, reports on the disputes against the 'butty system' and the role of the Barnsley men. The 'butty system' was where one man would sub contract others to work for him:

"Jack had to take on the butty men; they were bullies and he was very much on his own against them; he had to be strong to take them on. Then there were the Barnsley bullyboys; they weren't sympathetic to the union.

They sent over a manager from Chislet, Leavers, an ex-NCB boxing champion, so he'd have been a collier before. So they sent him over to deal with "Red Jack", they thought they would frighten him. So Leavers said, 'If we can't settle this here, we'll have to go out in the yard and take our jackets off and settle it there!' So Jack said, 'You had better get your jacket off now then!' But they reached an agreement and then there was mutual respect." (Janet Dunn, 2006)

A miners widow reports that she was always finding her husband suddenly at home and reports her husband as saying:

"This is the best pit, we've ever worked in. All the dregs, all the militants, all the Communists was all flung down there, so at the least excuse, they'd say, 'come on' and everyone came out of the pit!" (Mary Fowler, 2006)

Management provoked many disputes:

"The manager when Albert Welford started was Kiers, with his son as under manager; they lived at Finglesham. After him Mottershead; he was terrible; he used to rule with a heavy hand. If you took a day off the next day there would be a note saying your lamp would be stopped and you had to go and see him; he'd say, 'You can have another day off then.' His pal's wife had had a baby and stayed with her for the night, so Mottershead said he could take another one off (i.e. not be paid again)." (Albert Welford, 2006)

In the 1930s, the State applied a means test to anyone receiving benefits or 'relief'. This meant that if someone in your household was earning you could not claim social relief from the State. The means test carried out on Albert Welford's mother, in Leeds, counted Albert as part of the household and therefore rejected her claim, albeit he was 220 miles away in Kent. Albert had to help his mother by sending her ten shillings a week from his wages.

Some areas were particularly militant:

"The pan turners held the pit to ransom because if we didn't turn the pans, the colliers couldn't throw the coal. They refused to do what we called double chucking, throwing the coal over the track into the conveyor. I remember once about 1963 we went to the pit this Monday, there was a problem with the big dockets we used to get for the work we'd earned the week before. The Chargeman used to get them.

I heard there was trouble on 4's. The men said we aren't going to work until we've been paid the money we're due. That week I went home 5 times, gone down pit at 10 o'clock, riding at 11.30 and walking home, because the last buses was all gone. All the pan turners went out of the pit. " (Terry Birkett, 2006)

"You'd have a dispute – this is on the coalfaces and pan turning rippers. You'd have a dispute, say the timber was too long when it came in and you had to saw every one and you were spending a lot of time sawing props. You'd be losing money, so they'd say they were not going to pay you for that. You'd say ' sod it, rag up!' You'd have a meeting and just walk off. You'd crawl along and have a meeting in the gate, one end or the other. We had a lot when I was a pan turner;

Riding on West Paddy

we were walking the top road regular; if it was a nice day you'd walk across the brooks or sometimes you'd walk down the railway line. Pan turners was famous for rag ups… I remember one day we called 'rag up, lets have a meeting' and there was one guy, a market man who was on his way there to replace someone and we had the meeting and decided *not* to rag up. He arrived and said 'what d'you mean you're not ragging up, I've thrown my grub and water away' so we said 'sod it' and walked out!" (Dickie Prescott, 2006)

"We used to just refuse to work if it was unsafe, if there was too much dust, we'd demand water, just simple things. If something were dangerous we wouldn't work in it. If we were working in water up to our ankles, some of the officials would pay two of us and not pay me, then the next week they'd leave another out. So we'd say – either put it right or we're going home." (Peter Holden, 2006)

"They were always 'ragging up' all the time and almost always over money. Then there was a dispute over the shift times. There were 3 shifts: daytime, 2-10pm and nights. We wanted the afternoon shift to start earlier at 12 and finish at 8pm, so we could get to the pub. It wouldn't have reduced production, because we were suggesting the shift change happened at the pit bottom." (John Moyle, 2006)

Records of the Pit Production Committee in the 1940s give examples of the different kinds of dispute.

In only one week, in 1945, the following walkouts and sendings home by management were recorded:

"4th Nov- 22s; 4 men refused to work in bad area. 100s returned home saying 104s was their face. 22s & 24s went back – no safe travelling road. 6th Nov 64s men came out of their own accord, complained lumps of coal would not pass RH C/V engine. 76s came out 2 am – complained shortage of pressure for jigger picks. 96s sent out 2.30 am, fall at front rip. 104s sent out 4.25 am – face conveyor chain broken. 7th Nov 26s sent out after a workmen died in the pit. 64s, 26s, 76s, 104s, 19s & 17s not at work next day. 8th Nov 28s came out complained of blast engine trouble, which caused a lot of delay. 9th Nov 64s sent out 10.am – LH conveyor engine broke down and fall on RH face." (Pit production form, Ministry of Labour, 13th November 1945)

There were also disputes and claims over the payment of 'Essential Works Orders'. This was the name for payments that were made to men who were not able to do their normal work. They might take a form of dispute because buses were running late and people could not reach their normal work, or, as NUM Branch minutes reported, the '70s' men walked out after trouble had been experienced with the 'trunk conveyor'.

The union did not always support walkouts. The District Committee wrote on the 28th October 1946 to panmen at Betteshanger, reminding them that they should use the 'Conciliation Machinery'.

In a minute of a deputation by the union to management in November 1955:

> "Immediately after the installation of the belt on '10s'' jig, the layout of the pit was such that it led to an increased amount of waiting time. The contract had been adversely affected and the men considered the only way to focus attention on their problems was to walk out."

The union, in the person of Jack Dunn, signed an agreement that this was not to happen and that conciliation, either formally, or informally in the pit, was to be used to sort things out, so walk outs did not need to take place.

On the 17th August 1956, management, the National Union of Colliery Overmen, Deputies and Shotfirers (NACODS), the Deputies Union and the National Union of Mineworkers (NUM), signed a memo saying that in response to, 'cases where, following disagreement with an official workmen have not carried out work on a particular shift, conciliation should take place without a stoppage.'

It wasn't the Union Branch at those times that principally lead the disputes; they were lead by the workforce, who might have to explain themselves to the Branch committee:

> "I'd have to go before the Branch Committee and there were 5/6 of us

and Joe Burke was having a go and they were all caving in around me – you'd look round and all the heads would be on the floor and under the table and I was the only one still standing there!" (John Moyle, 2006)

"The Managers tried to put them down, but the committee in the Union at Betteshanger was outstanding. I've always said the men were the Union, but the committee was outstanding. The Chairman and the secretaries, no matter what problem the men had you could go to them and they'd help you solve it quite quickly." (Joe Dickenson, 2006)

Miners who broke the European production record

But the branch committee did normally support the men:

"We did have a problem at Betteshanger when management thought they were far superior to the workforce, but that got virtually stopped. I was a Charge hand on a team and we used to walk out of the pit fairly often and very rarely did we not get the money back and 9 times out of 10 we was right. The management used to send different officials onto the district; trying to curb us. We wasn't doing anything wrong and we'd walk out many a time and the Branch didn't mind and the management team they kept saying (to the Manager) 'you're too weak to deal with them, we'll send someone else', but it kept getting worse. Because of the likes of Johnny Moyle and Terry Harrison, we knew we had them in the background, I was proud to be part of that.

We'd walk out over pay, conditions – they'd say 'your water money is stopped'. It was no good saying that to our team, we'd say 'alright don't pay us' and we'd walk out. Deep down we knew the committee would get it back for us. We always done the work, one day we broke the record for production of all the coalface. We were known throughout the coalfield – Twenties.

First nationalised coal at Betteshanger

They got so militant the management couldn't stop them, they tried everything to break them, but they couldn't, they were so militant because of their background."
(Joe Dickenson, 2006)

Such militancy had it's roots in their collective history.

Nationalisation

Life before and after nationalisation may appear little different. But many older miners speak of the difference nationalisation made. Vesting day, with the first nationalised coal, was a proud moment. This was the day that ownership of the coal mines was transferred from the coal owners and vested in the people.

After nationalisation there was a glowing report on the industry and the Minister of Fuel and Power, Mannny Shinwell, opened Betteshanger training centre saying:

"This is an honourable, interesting, secure, well-paid industry. For too long it has been disparaged."

Waiting to ride the paddy

But the honeymoon was brief. In the Evening News of Sept 29th 1948, there was a report that 2,000 Betteshanger miners were threatened with the sack and closure of the pit.

The branch committee still wanted all disputes to go through them. The branch also discussed matters such as dust problems and a panmen's dispute. But at the same time the branch was discussing international issues such as opposing troops going to Indo China, the Governments policy on Greece and conducted a levy in favour of the International Brigade.

Whilst miners wanted to produce coal, there were proud moments when one team exceeded production records, the pattern of 'rag ups' and disputes starting unofficially on the coalface, sometimes supported by the branch committee and sometimes not, were common in every decade at the pit.

We now turn back in time a little to look at the famous 1942 strike.

SIXTY YEARS OF STRUGGLE

THE 1942 WARTIME STRIKE

4

The Betteshanger miners on strike had a ditty to accompany the action:

> *"So, Mr Bevin, we ask you please*
> *To take our case before Magees*
> *We know the country's short of coal*
> *But 6/9d's worse than the dole"*

(Mass Observation, wartime social survey, 1942)

The renowned 1942 Wartime strike at Betteshanger is well known as the time and place where militant miners successfully defied the law.

For some it suggested a lack of patriotism or commitment to a war against fascist dictatorship. But for the Kent miners the battle at home against wage-cutting managers was a battle against local dictatorship.

In this chapter we look at the wartime context and background to the strike. How the strike progressed through the imprisonment and release of it's leaders, together with the role of the Communist Party.

The War Context

The location of Betteshanger Colliery, near Deal on the East Kent coast, put it in the front line facing bombardment. German bombers either on their way to London or, on their way back, still with bombs on board, had their last opportunity to hit British targets before they left the Kent coast. The pit, with its role in wartime production of coal was a particular target and was hit twice.

"The Gerry's came over this morning and bombed the pit. We shall not be starting work for a good while now."

"More bombs dropped in the town."

"As we were about to go down, the Luftwaffe came over and planted a bomb right through the winding house (did not go off). Not able to work' (Wilf Aldred diary, 1942)

Ross Llewellyn in his book (Hersden: Chislet Colliery, Village 2003) records that there were 2,500 air raids at that Kent pit. A pit further from the coast than Betteshanger. During the battle of Britain alerts might last 14 hours, during which, at Chislet, it is recorded that winding stopped; if you were down you stayed down.

Miners who went down the pit knew that their wives and children were facing the bombing above. The miners in Kent were facing danger, as were their families. Not being aware of the situation above ground caused a great deal of tension.

Because of the bombing, East Kent was an area of civilian evacuation. The Mines Department held a meeting to discuss what would happen in the event of invasion. A provision was noted: 'The evacuation scheme provides for removal of all residents to the outskirts of London'.
(9th August 1941)

Mary Fowler followed her husband south, after he was black listed in Fife. Joe Burke (later NUM branch secretary) came too and lodged with them. She remembers:

"When I got to Deal (1941) I thought it was a ghost town. It was like the Wild West with nobody there. My God, people had run away, been evacuated and left everything." (Mary Fowler, 2006)

There were some problems of how to stop men leaving the area when women and children had been evacuated.

The Ministry of Mines recorded that in 1940 the Government discussed mothballing the Kent pits, but realised this was not possible because of the need for coal. It was seen as very important to maintain production in Kent because, if bombing disrupted railways, Kent was the only source of coal south of Thames.

> "For this reason the mines department regard maintenance of maximum output in Kent as of great strategic importance.
>
> It is submitted that none of the men at present engaged at any of the 4 collieries should be called up." (Page Arnot, Historian of the Miners, 1949)

The Mine Workers Federation Union records reveal that between 1941 and 1944 there were problems with the threat of invasion and recruitment of additional labour, as they could not move other miners to Kent.

> "The underground conditions in Kent pits are such that men from other districts, where conditions are not similar, do not readily adapt themselves to the Kent pits." (Mineworkers Federation, Dover Archive, 1941)

In addition, Deal was in earshot of German heavy artillery in France, almost on the front line. Miners came forward with bedding and clothes for the troops returning from Dunkirk. The town was full of soldiers, as Mary Fowler reports:

> "I used to hurry home before the blackout and a soldier would lift the bairn onto his shoulders and run with him to help you. Soldiers used to knock on your door because they knew they were going across to France to get killed. They'd say 'I've got a carpet'. I said 'I have nae Hoover'. They said, 'I'll get you a hoover!'" (Mary Fowler, 2006)

This was the difficult environment in which Betteshanger miners, and those of other Kent pits, were working. Management chose not to make allowances for these external difficulties and did not act to achieve consensus in the face of the wartime dangers.

Management Provocation

Relations between men and management were not good and the latter's behaviour continued to be provocative. In early August 1941, they put up a notice, signed by Mr. Johnson the Manager, with reference to the stoppage of '18s" coal face. The men went on strike in protest over the 4d that had been stopped from their wages.

The notice read:

> "The Management wish to point out that as a result 32 tons of coal were lost to the country at a time when our soldiers, airmen and sailors are fighting for your lives. The management have reason for thinking therefore that patriotic men allowed themselves to be influenced by one or two 5th columnists who are set out to hinder production."

The Union's response was predictable and a reply was posted on the 11th August:

> "Strong exception was taken to the notice... I was instructed to inform you that unless you substantiate your accusation, or post an apology, failing this, legal opinion will be sought with a view to taking the matter further.' Signed, George Daughtrey, Branch Secretary, Betteshanger Kent Mine Workers Association (KMWA)." (Union Records, East Kent Archive, Dover, 1941)

The 1942 Strike

In accounts of the dispute there is a view that greedy miners were jeopardising the nation by their actions. But the strike can be seen as caused by the behaviour of the management. In particularly a Mr Magee, as referred to in the ditty reported by Mass Observation.

The wartime social surveyists had an observer, VT, in Deal, who, like all Mass Observation people on the ground, remains anonymous. He or she reported that:

> "Manager McGee was 'a very tough proposition, disliked by men' and even a local pub landlord said he was hard. He came from Featherstone (a non Union pit) in Yorkshire and had kept men on strike there for 2½ year, even turning women and kids from homes onto street and is reported that he had said from the start he was 'going to smash the Union' at Betteshanger." (Mass Observation)

In November 1941, 1,000 men had started a go-slow over a pay dispute. The Ministry of Mines Arbitrator came to adjudicate:

> "That old fellow they sent down knew about as much about a coal mine as my dog did. He collapsed with the heat when we went down the mine" (Joe Methuen, later imprisoned miners' leader, reported in the Sunday Times, 28th February 1971)

> "The reason for the strike was it was a new seam and the J seam, and it was difficult, the floors were blowing and it was hot. They were being paid 10/6d a shift, and the manager, Mr. McGee said that if you make this work I'll pay you 12/3d and he went back on it. People said that it was terrible striking in wartime, but when you heard the whole story it's different." (Dickie Prescott, 2006)

> " 'Either we get the normal wage or we strike', said Joe Methuen. 'They flatly refused and we said that's it, the wheel's won't turn on Monday'." (Sunday Times, 28th February 1971)

This led to a 19-day strike by 2,000 in January 1942, which was in breach of the wartime emergency regulations obliging compulsory arbitration.

The local union pointed out:

> "Betteshanger has been a pit renowned for its fighting qualities in the defence of wages and conditions." (KMWA)

The National Union had a different view. On the 10th June 1940, a letter to all districts from Ebby Edwards read:

> "Strikes or lockouts cannot be permitted when the enemy are at the gates. …Lightening and unconstitutional stoppages of every kind must be abolished."

Wilf Aldred was a member of the Communist Party at the time. He was an underground worker, went away to join the RAF in 1942 and returned to the pit as a deputy. His diary describes life just before the start of the strike:

> *Thursday 1st January 1942.*
> "Went with J&D to see Bing Crosby in the 'Eastside of Heaven'. I also changed my library books."

> *Friday 2nd January.*
> "Went to Deal, I bought 2 records of Bing Crosby 'Stardust'"

> *Saturday 3rd January.*
> "In the evening J & I went for a walk, then we went to a dance at St.Leonard's.
> 'I went to see about my Income Tax. I fixed J's gramophone and we played our favourite song 'Stardust'"

> *Friday 9th January.*
> "We came out on strike today, so I did not go to work. Went to the Library to change our books. We then went to see 'The Big Breakfast' at the Odeon.'"

The Mass Observation Observer, in Deal at the time, made the following notes:

> "Disputes about wages had been going on since before Christmas, but the men only decided to strike when the management *cut* the day wages of about 40 men working on a particular coal face from 10/4 halfpenny to 7/-, giving no notice of the intention and consequently

breaking the minimum wage expectation. Thus the talk was that it was not unpatriotic they *had* to do it (strike). One man referring to the fact that strikes are illegal in wartime said, 'It is like the Nazis isn't it?'.

The feeling was of a 'very strong hate, a sense of injustice, a fear of having their whole standard of life made much more difficult to achieve, that is making them so determined to go through with this fight whatever it entails.' They speak of how Magee had never been beaten before." (VT, Mass Observation, 17th-18th January1942)

Wilf Aldred describes progress of the strike:

Wednesday 14th January.
"We are still on strike; there are no hopes of settling it. We went out for a walk in the morning and got plenty of fresh air."

Thursday 15th January.
"There was a meeting today, but we never reached anything as far as going back to work. D and I spent the afternoon chopping trees down."

Friday 16th January.
"There was also a meeting this morning, everything is at a deadlock. All the boys walked it to the pit, to draw out money, it will be the last we shall draw for a long time."

The owners and Ministry of Mines decided to prosecute, which brought its own headaches. A Sunday Times article reported:

"The Chief Constable of Kent didn't have enough forms we had to scratch around getting them from the Home Office and the Stationery Office." (28th February 1941)

Extra Justices of the Peace had to be found to sign all 1000 forms – in duplicate, naturally, and extra Police were drafted in to serve them. Joe Methuen remembers the day his summons arrived. He recalled: 'There was one chap supposed to have been prosecuted, but they gave it to his brother by mistake'.

Saturday 17th January.
"We all got served with a summons today and have to appear at Canterbury on 23rd. D & I went to the evening classes at Canterbury and to the dance in the evening after classes." (Wilf Aldred)

The Ministry of Labour's problems accumulated. News of the prosecutions had spread to other coalfields. Their miners decided to express their solidarity with the Betteshanger men by sending representatives. They even sent colliery bands to Canterbury on the day of the hearing.

Three officials were sentenced to hard labour and the remainder of the men were fined £1, each with the option of jail for non-payment. The men refused to pay the fine, or return to work, until the three officials had been released from Maidstone prison.

Tudor Davies, one of the imprisoned

Thursday 22nd January.
"There was a ballot today to see if we should go back to work or not. Everybody voted against it, so we are still on strike. Suits me."

Friday 23rd January.
"We were all tried who were on strike and got fined £1. Our Secretary was put in jail for two months and two other of our leaders got one month

each. I suppose we will not be long at following them, because they will never get a pound off me or anyone else." (Wilf Aldred Diary)

Joe Methuen described life in prison:

"We were picking oakum and sewing bags and when we whispered to each other the warder would growl, 'Not so much bloody talk'. To eat, we had a drop of skilly with a piece of bread, with a bit of margarine and a bit of cheese as big as a sugar cube, and porridge with no milk or sugar, and cocoa the same. It was bloody awful." (Sunday Times, 1971)

But Joe Methuen's discomfort was equalled by that of Sir Harold Emmerson at the Ministry of Labour. 'When the news got out', he says, 'there were protests all over the miners' world. The imprisoned men were quickly becoming martyrs'. The Ministry of Labour were becoming concerned at the widening impact on war production. (Sunday Times, 1971)

Mass Observation detailed how difficult it was to cope while on strike. In summer, it would be so much easier. But now coal was running short and as most of the households cook, as well as heat, by coal, this was very serious.

"On Saturday there was a stream of men going the 2 miles to Walmer with sacks to get a bag of coke, at 2/3d a bag, a price which they could ill afford. Some wheeled hand barrows, others balanced sacks on bicycle seats. Someone reported that during the last couple of weeks they had chopped up the two chairs from their Anderson shelter, torn up the whole of the floor and used it board by board, done the same to the door and on Sunday night were removing the final doorpost.

In the last strike there wasn't a shelf left anywhere in the houses, and someone remembered a strike in Northumberland where the miners were in new Council houses, and there wasn't a picture rail left after it!

The food situation is not bad yet in most families. Most of the wives are getting the relief tickets, 12/6d for a wife and 4/- for the first 2 children, 3/- per child after that. This amount just about buys the essential groceries and meat ration.

The sentence of hard labour passed on Tudor Davies who is a JP and very well thought of, is considered harsh and there is a feeling of injustice about the whole proceedings. There are now a good many allusions to Russia and the attitude of Managements towards her."
(Mass Observation, 1942)

Wilf Aldred continues:

Sunday 25th January.
"There was a meting this morning and it was said that we were not starting work until our leaders came out of jail."

Monday 26th January.
"There was a meeting between the Unions and owners but everything is at deadlock. J took me to the pictures, we saw 'Billy the Kid' I then went across the Welfare to a free dance."

Tuesday 27th January.
"There was another meeting between the Union and the Company. The Minister of the Mines and the Secretary of the Mines were there and it looks as if they will settle the strike."

Mass Observation reported on one of the meetings:

"Two of the representatives on the platform were saying go back to work and wait for more arbitration, ' we're not bloody going back till pay's put back in those packets'; they bloody near got pulled off the platform, those two. They was shouted off, He also said that representatives were going to the Government and an appeal was being made against the sentences passed on the three in jail. A telegram was received from Scottish miners to say they were in support of the strike, and Billy Powell had had telegrams and money sent to him."

Wilf takes up the story:

> *Wednesday 28th January.*
> "The strike was settled today <u>in our favour</u>. We agreed to go back because he has paid the men what he owed them. The Minister of Mines was at the meeting. He is going to try to get our leaders out of jail."

> *Thursday 29th January.*
> "I started work this morning again. I had a pretty good shift. There was a free dance tonight at the Welfare. We are having some pretty cold weather."

At this occasion several people report McGee buying everyone drinks. It cost him £160.

> "After it was over he went up to the Welfare and he said he'd buy every man a drink and they all went for expensive drinks, not all 10d pints, they all went for Whiskies, the dearest drinks in the place!" (Dickie Prescott, 2006)

There was widespread support both from the women in the community and more widely. Councillor Mrs. Mantle, whose husband was on strike, said:

> "The women are solidly behind the men because convinced owners are attacking the minimum wage." (East Kent Gazette, 1942)

After 11 weeks of mass demonstrations, the government waived the fines and released the Union officials.

The Implications of the Strike

In an extract from my 1987 PhD thesis, I endeavour to describe the situation:

The Ministry of Labour received the largest number of letters of protest during the war about these prosecutions from Labour Party branches, Shop Stewards, Committees, Unions and the NCCL and Peace Pledge Union. The following letter was typical:

'The harsh treatment of these miners will only serve to weaken the efforts of all sections of the working class and will have a serious effect on the national effort. I earnestly beseech you, in common with many other working class mothers to release the three miners of Betteshanger colliery and withdraw the fines from the other miners, which no working class home can afford and means great hardship of the mothers and children.

These miners so harshly sentenced have kept the mines at full production, often during raids and when bombs have been dropping. Many of the strikers in spite of their arduous work are members of the Home Guard, and have all been doing their bit, while the public still purchase black-market goods and those selling on the black-market continue their evil doing, often paying fines which would mean nothing to the wealthy, whereas a fine in any miner's home is the children's bread.

Hoping you will consider the matter favourably to the miners involved. Yours respectfully concluded. Marcia Mandalstrat.' (LAB 10 204 (Reference number for Ministry of Labour Archive, National Archive, Kew))

The state intervened in industrial relations through conscription, regulations such as the Essential Works Order, preventing employers sacking workers and workers leaving, and most crucially, through Order 1305 which prohibited strikes. This prohibition of strikes was a failure. Indeed from 1941, until the order was revoked in 1951, strikes were considerably more frequent than in any of the preceding years.

The Ministry of Labour admitted:

"The settlement at Betteshanger amounted, practically to a complete surrender to the men, even though there may be apparently safeguarding words in the agreement, we had hoped and had been led to believe, that no concessions would be made unless and until the men returned to work. This principle is of great importance because otherwise there is encouragement to widespread stoppage and refusal to work until satisfactory terms have been reached. This is likely to embarrass Trade Union officials as much as ourselves. The whole position is most unfortunate and it will not help in preventing strikes or enforcing the prohibition of strikes in the future." (LAB 10 187: Ministry of Labour Archive, National Archive, Kew)

D Parkin. Nation, Class and Gender in Second World War Britain. Thesis. LSE 1987.

Role of the Communist Party

Given the history of the influence of the Communist Party in supporting miners' education and taking a leading role in the union at Betteshanger, their role in the 1942 strike is interesting.

The Soviet Union had ended the Stalin Hitler pact in June 1941 and was entirely behind the war. This meant that the Communist Party wholeheartedly supported the war effort. As confirmed in a personal communication, this was to the extent of sending Communists, such as Olive Currie down a pit in Wales to agitate for increased war production.

But the strike at Betteshanger was so widely supported that it was hard for the Communist Party to stand out against it.

In 1942 we can find no direct evidence of their attitude to the strike. We may speculate that there must have been conflicting motives. Some in the country saw strike action as unpatriotic and against the war effort.

At a time when the Communist Party were fully supporting the war effort with the rallying call, 'Remember Mother Russia', supporting the workers in strike action must have felt compromising. In either case, Communist Party member, Wilf Aldred showed no reservations in his support for the strike.

Mass Observation reported people saying:

> "'What are we fighting for, to help Russia win the war or keep the bloody owners rich? 'Call this a democracy? This war's no good to the working men; there's plenty of rich folk making money out of it?' 'They call Russia an ally, while she's winning the war for us but you wait till after, then they'll turn round'."

The strike was so overwhelmingly popular locally that the Communist Party did not, or could not, speak against it.

Their underlying attitude was however expressed a year later when miners at Betteshanger and Snowdown threatened strike action for the same reasons as in 1942, as management began to threaten a reduction in prices (wages).

The Kent District Committee of the Communist Party wrote to John Elkes, the secretary of the Kent Miners Association, on 11th November 1943:

> "It is clear that the Management of these collieries has made an attack on prices and agreements which have been operating for many years and have shown they are not interested in the uninterrupted production of coal so vital at the present stage of the war."

The Communist Party goes on to say that the owners can be forced to restore the cuts:

> "…through the recognised machinery, the force of public opinion and pressure from the Labour movement."

And that the employer's provocation could be stopped:

"Without the tragedy of a stoppage of work at the two collieries, which would be harmful to the vital struggle against Hitler, the worst enemy the working class have ever had to face."

They said that a resolution on these lines had been passed by:

- Cray Valley AEU.
- 8 & 9 Branches of Crayford AEU.
- Dartford and District Branch of the Plumbers and Domestic Engineers Union.
- West Kent committee of the National Union of Agricultural Workers.

A letter from the West Kent Union of Agricultural Workers, dated 6th November 1943, is also in the NUM files at Dover:

"We support the KMWA in their stand on this provocation by the employers which is against the national interest and can only lead to reduced production of coal so vital to the carrying on of the war to speedy victory."

It would not have been popular for the Communist Party to oppose the strike in 1942, but they argued and mobilised strongly against proposed strikes over the same issue in 1943.

Many say that the role of the Communist Party was contradictory; they were excellent at educating miners in political history and economics and at organising campaigns on international issues.

There was a view that the key thing for the Communist Party was to be popular in order to win positions as Branch officers in the union. Thus it was not possible to oppose the 1942 strike, notwithstanding the Communist Party's national position of support for the war once the Stalin Hitler pact was no more.

The 1942 illegal strike at Betteshanger has since that time stood as an example of the difficulties of prosecuting workers for striking. The strike was provoked by management and, despite the war, Betteshanger miners were not prepared to accept a cut in their wage rates. Their tradition of militancy coming down from 1926, and through the strikes in the 1930s, meant they were not prepared to be put upon and accept injustice even during the war.

(We acknowledge, with thanks, the help of Trustees of the Mass Observation Archive, University of Sussex. Quotes are from Mass Observation Observer VT (anon.), 26th January 1942, 64/2/A: Survey of a Strike at Betteshanger Colliery)

THE 1960 STAY DOWN STRIKE   5

After the war, even with nationalisation, industrial relations pretty much reverted back to the patterns of the 1930s. However, in the late 1950s, matters came to a head once more.

It is clear that the National Coal Board (NCB) had commenced a policy of retraction of the coal industry from 1958.

In April of that year, John Plumptree, Divisional General Manager of the NCB, wrote to Jack Dunn, the area secretary of the NUM, about 'certain fears about the future of number 6 seam' at Betteshanger. He wanted to discuss, 'the whole question of manpower and recruitment in Kent.' (Letter, East Kent Archive, 3rd April 1958)

The Board itself published a document 'Prospects for 1959'. It stated that because it was a difficult time they might need to restrict recruitment. They referred to the competition from oil consumption, which had gone from 8.1 million tons per year in 1955, to an estimated 14.5 million tons in 1958. They argued:

> "It seems inescapable that this must be dealt with by a reduction in deep mine production." ('Prospects for 1959', NCB, Dover Archive)

They said that 'any redundancy that arises will be minimised' and threatened closures only of uneconomic pits, none of which were in Kent. They also spoke of encouraging over 65's to retire, in order 'to make room for younger men from closed collieries'

They were seeking a reduction in deep mine coal of 3 million tons a year. (NCB, East Kent Archive, December 1958)

Goffee reports:

> "After 1956 a flood of cheap foreign oil undercut the price of British coal... The NCB opted to contract numbers employed in order to improve productivity and restore the market position of coal." (1978)

It would not be until 1970 that the price of oil began to rise and by 1973 was actually expensive. From that date there were plans to expand the coal industry.

The Stay Down Strike

In January 1960, management made the decision to sack 120 young miners at Betteshanger. At this time the number seven seam was being exhausted.

Protests outside the NCB, Hobart House

THE 1960 STAY DOWN STRIKE

Terry Harrison describes it:

> "At Betteshanger, the pit was the predominate employer in the area. There was an endemic unemployment problem, right around the coast, because it was also the start of the decline in traditional British holidays. So whereas you had Margate, Folkestone, Broadstairs, previously the place for annual holidays for the Midlands and things like that, that had started to decline too, So there was this endemic unemployment problem and the Branch perceived that they couldn't risk contracting of the pits... There were decisions made that the branch should oppose the sackings of young miners, because it was last in first out, the policy of most Unions then." (2006)

In response to these sackings came the stay down strike, the night shift remaining in the pit. Some men from the day shift joined them.

The Communist party had discussed the proposed strike. Janet Dunn reports it was planned in their front room. Other rank and file leaders such as Arnold Moyle, John Moyle's father, and Barney Wynne were also involved:

> "It was rank and file and it was visited on the branch really."
> (Terry Harrison, 2006)

John Moyle was one of the sacked young miners

> "They had sacked about 160 of us – it was 'last in first out' and all of us young ones were sacked. So they started the stay down strike; my father Arnold Moyle, was one of the leaders. He was on night shift and they stayed down and when the day shift came down they kept them down too. No-one was going to argue with it – it was one out, all out, that was how it was." (John Moyle, 2006)

One of the interviewees, not himself a militant, describes it:

> "We knew this strike was coming off; I was off sick with an injured hand. And the next night on 4s, they were all Communists, bar three

Carrying food to the stay down strikers

of us' they would join the party in and out, not the Catholics, they wouldn't join, but they were still militant. The Union went down 4s I was told and said - 'look lads we want you to stay down the pit because we'll bring them quickly to their knees. The day shift came down but all they did was give their snap to the night shift who were down there, they didn't stay down." (Dickie Prescott, 2006)

According to the local paper, the strike started at 10pm, Wednesday 10th February. 377 miners, who were fit and did not have serious domestic commitments, decided to stay down. This was later reduced to 135 because of the difficulties of feeding them all.

One of our informants wrote anonymously to us. He was a Shaftsman who kept working to bring food supplies down to the men in the pit:

"My first recollection is of the vast amount of material that night after night we took down the pit. Hundreds of blankets, coats, pullovers, socks and other clothing to help keep the men warm, for with the fans still working drawing cold air into the mine, even on the normally warm side of the pit, it was quite cold."

"Food? It was amazing, the variety and the abundance. There was fried chicken, beef stew, sandwiches by the hundreds, and even fish and chips. There was chocolate, nuts, crisps and hot flasks of tea, probably laced with something a bit stronger. Also, a mouth organ and false teeth…"

A local paper talks of a certain Mr Jack Ford, who was ordered to leave the pit by strike leaders due to the severity of his silicosis. He immediately returned home, killed seven hens, roasted them and sent them to the pit.

There was a postal service daily from the start, including 200 Valentines:

"Messages sent to the men by their loves ones all had the same words of encouragement. Stick it out; we're with you and we won't let you down." (The Shaftsman, 2006)

There was even music played and the press were told the story that Joe Dickenson had been playing skiffle down the pit.

Our Shaftsman recalled:

"At times, it would be fairly quiet, the men sleeping or quietly talking. At other times an impromptu concert would be taking place with an appreciative but rowdy audience shouting encouragement, to the singers, the storytellers and the jokers. The men seemed to have lost all notion of time. They ate when they felt like eating; they slept intermittently, and often the concerts would be taking place at 3 or 4 in the morning. They would amuse themselves by bunging stones at cockroaches, or constructing elaborate traps to catch the mice."

The local paper explains that St Johns Ambulance went down and told them to exercise, so they have been doing 3-mile walks along dusty underground roadways in the pit. Lenny Lenthall, Southern Counties Light Heavyweight Boxing Champion, kept fit by training down the pit. He even sent for his skipping rope.

The local paper said no one needed medical attention after they came up:

> " 'But some of them complained their eyes smarted.' Gordon Nicholls said, 'I would have stopped down there for a month if the Union had not ordered me up...my only ill effects are that my eyes are a bit sore and my chest is a bit rough, but that's with too much singing, playing games & sing songs!' " (East Kent Gazette, 1960)

There were some Catholics amongst those who stayed down and there was a request to allow a priest down on the Sunday to conduct Mass. Management refused this. But the Catholic priest Father P MacGuinness didn't mind the refusal. The paper reported:

> "I am against the strikers actions, so I did not mind."

Driving a new roadway

There was a march to NCB offices in Dover with a banner, 'Herr Plumtree, the hypocritical dictator, who banned the clergy from Betteshanger'

Les Magness, the NUM branch secretary, addressed the demo. He announced that he knew:

" ...that Betteshanger had given a headache to many people in the coal board but Betteshanger will not work for nothing. All that we ask is the right to work and that is the right for every British freeborn man. But we are not slaves, we will not be dictated to."

From left to right: Lester Magness and Joe Burke

Joe Burke roused the crowd:

"Remember everyone in the country has an equal share in Betteshanger. It is owned by the public... at this moment no doubt Mr Plumtree is sitting in his comfortable office with a smug smile on his face. The longest our men have been held in pit before was 171 hours in 1942 when 3 bombs dropped in pit yard. As Hitler failed, we are determined you should fail... We are many Mr Plumtree, you are few. One day the pits will belong to us."

National organising and the end of the strike

During the stay down, as in the 1942 strike and earlier disputes, delegations were sent throughout the country. They went back to the miners' coalfields of origin to organise support.

"You, Jock go back to Fife. The Welsh to Wales and so on."
(Terry Birkett, 2006)

This was the legacy of the pits' origins. Having been filled mainly by militant miners, black listed from other areas, Betteshanger men retained their personal connections with militants from their old coalfields and were able to draw upon their support.

Eventually, on the 28th February 1960, after 18 days of stay down, the Branch recommended a return:

> "...on giving the promise that the National Officials, Jones & Paynter should be 'invited to the area to open up discussions on the issue of redundancy.'" (Branch Minutes)

A strike committee minute said they were:

> "Aware of the financial position of our Union's funds and realise that the area have undertaken to pay 2 week's strike pay only; in these circumstances we are reluctantly compelled to recommend an immediate resumption of work with the unqualified pledge to do our uttermost to see that the 140 are re-absorbed in the Kent pits as soon as possible and that no workmen will be signed on at

Meeting the February cold with blankets, a brass band and cigarettes

60

Betteshanger until everyone of those men had the opportunity to return." (NUM Betteshanger Branch Minute, East Kent Archive, 28th February 1960)

When they came up, a brass band played and they were welcomed as heroes. Big blankets were thrown over them against the February cold and John Moyle remembers standing and handing out cigarettes (Players Weights) to them as they emerged.

Our Shaftsman concluded:

"Night after night we Shaftsman were privileged to see it as it happened and speaking on behalf of my mates, most of whom are no longer with us, I can only say: We salute you." (Letter, 2006)

On 14th March 1960, Joe Burke wrote to Jack Dunn, the Area Secretary, saying that 80 of 140 miners were still unemployed, with 56 not getting any redundancy. He pointed out that the pit was short of 15 colliers and rippers. Further more, these colliers and rippers had been down graded to doing clearing up in the gate (doing the jobs of the sacked). The belt had broken twice and colliers had to be taken off the face to repair it.

"It is a happy happy home at present, with the lid likely to blow off anytime." (Letter, J Burke, East Kent Archive, 14th March 1960)

John Moyle, like others, found different employment. He found work at a dairy in London but by August he was back at Betteshanger.

The significance of this dispute was that it made clear to the management that despite industrial retraction they could not make men redundant. The NUM was a force to be reckoned with, and their militant practice continued. Adding to it's traditions, this was the first stay down strike at Betteshanger and was to be repeated in 1984.

A young collier 1963, Betteshanger

THE STRIKES OF 1972 AND 1974 AND OTHER ACTION

6

These two disputes were national strikes over wages and conditions, therefore the story of Kent is a part of a national picture. This UK wide picture has had many accounts published. Indeed, the Kent story has also been told in Malcolm Pitt's work 'The World on Our Backs'. Pitt was later to be NUM Kent Area President for a brief time.

The BBC web page 'On this day', sets the scene. On the 9th January 1972:

> "Coal miners walked out at midnight in their first national strike for almost 50 years. Three months of negotiations with the National Coal Board ended in deadlock four days ago with an offer of 7.9% on the table and the promise of a backdated deal for an increase in productivity. The 280,000 mineworkers signalled their determination to break the Government's unofficial eight per cent pay ceiling... They are looking for an increase of up to £9 a week - on an average take home wage of £25.
>
> Miners have been observing an overtime ban since 1st November in support of their pay claim, which the NCB estimates has already cost the industry £20m."

Terry Harrison gives the local angle on the 1972 strike:

> "Betteshanger was already enjoying the highest wage levels in Kent and this was highest level of wages in Britain. One of the wishes of the union was that there would be a National Wage Structure.
>
> From the point of view of the Union, they got the day wage pay structure which was universal across the pits and this was for all of the outside workers, surface workers, fitters, electricians... They

Demonstration in London

had a problem with technical staff; they were the best-trained men, from the point of view that they was having to compete with other industries. Our problem was we couldn't retain them because we were paying them peanuts. So between the National Union and the Coal Board. They signed the National Power Loading Agreement (NPLA) Agreement, but incorporated the electricians and the fitters, quite rightly, as they should never have been in the situation they were. The other thing that it made was a promise to supervisory staff, National Association of Overmen and Deputies (NACODS) and other unions that at some stage they would be paid 10% more than a production worker. The NPLA also ended the disparity of wages in areas.

THE STRIKES OF 1972 AND 1974, AND OTHER ACTION

The Benchmark that the NPLA would be set on was the Nottinghamshire rate. The Nottinghamshire rate was just below the Kent rate, which was the highest rate.

The thing was for many of the people when the National Power Loading agreement came in, it was a great Socialist concept, but in reality many men were going to loose quite a lot. I am talking about 20-25%, so it wasn't chicken feed! But the other thing was that Kent knew that they would be standing still for many years to come. But the part of the agreement was that parity would be reached by either 1971 or 1972." (2006)

The reality was, that over the next five years, Kent only received a wage rise of 6d, 1/, or 1/6- a week.

The BBC web page report continued:

"The General Secretary of the National Union of Mineworkers, Lawrence Daly, has predicted coal stocks will quickly run down. 'Industrialists in this country will be pressing the Government to get the door open for serious talks,' He added, 'Three-quarters of the electricity used in the United Kingdom comes from coal-burning power stations. The strike comes at a time when the stations are facing long periods of peak demand during the cold weather.'"

The records in the South Wales Miners' Library reveal:

"At first the miners picketed at coal power stations, but then it was decided to target *all* power stations, and also steelworks, ports, coal depots and other major coal users. In South Wales, Dockers at Newport and Cardiff supported the miners by refusing to unload coal from ships. On the 21st January, the NUM decided to try to stop the movement of all fuel supplies. Miners from South Wales were involved in the pickets at the Saltley Marsh Coal Depot of the West Midlands Gas Board."

Our contributors explained their attitude to the strike:

"In the 1972 strike. I voted for it, I had only just come back to the mine and there was a lot of bitterness about the wages." (Dickie Prescott, 2006)

"In 1972 of course Betteshanger was well known, we created the flying pickets and got support and this was the winning part of that dispute." (Peter Holden, 2006)

My personal experience of Betteshanger miners started at this time. I first met miners in 1972, on picket lines at Dover docks, where there was violence from the scab lorry drivers who threatened pickets, including supporting students from the University of Kent, with an iron bar. The local paper reported that a Mr. Raymond Clutton was struck on the head by a lorry driver using an iron bar and was hospitalised.

I remember coming to Magness House (Hillside House it was then) during the 1972 strike and listening to a miner talking with great bitterness about the conditions in the pit, the heat, dust and water. He explained to the naïve, wide eyed, student I was, that of course there were no toilet facilities in the pit and you would squat where you were, with the stench that might follow. There was no way of washing hands and there was the possibility of putting your hand where someone else had been.

He also told me how much wages had declined, as Terry Harrison outlined earlier.

Kent, and in particular Betteshanger, as we would expect, played a leading role in organising picketing. Dickie Tank and others described to me how they organised picketing of the southeast from Hillside House (now Magness House), in Mill Hill, with a huge map of power stations and coal yards:

"The 1972 and 74 strikes were very similar, were over the same issues and it is hard to tell them apart in memory. But we learnt from 1972 and we was very well organised. We had a big map with pins in it of every coal yard, every power station all along the south coast and right through to the Isle of Grain. We'd just get sent out every day, there was no one at home during the strikes." (John Moyle, 2006)

"By the time we got into 1972 conflict, we was well organised. We were quickly onto the ground, but the important thing of 1972, was the policy of the TUC, the question of their members not crossing the picket lines. Now that really was the key to everything, because it meant that no

Demonstration in London

sooner had we got lads to the power stations, the picket lines were being honoured. That was the situation on rail, there were these two twins, they had a tent, there was a train of coal on the railway line at Medway and that train stopped there until the end of the strike, the train was there and it was pulled up at their picket line and that was it, it never moved." (Terry Harrison, 2006)

Betteshanger miners also participated in national demonstrations in London. They gradually became very media savvy with some eye-catching ideas, as Terry Harrison explains:

"The other one was that we had some fiascos that I remember, we was going to have a Miner's Navy and we was very slow learning, but something you pick up almost immediately with the media, as long as they could get a story, they couldn't give a monkey whether it was basically true or not! So, the Miner's Navy, we was going to get a boat off Clive Jenkins. The boat never come, so eventually the Miners Navy was actually launched on the back of a boat at Westminster pier – he had hired the boat and there we had got Harold Jones who was an organiser, come down from Bedworth, in Coventry and he shouted out messages to Battersea Power Station over his megaphone! -'Come in Battersea Power Station, this is the Miners picket boat'!"

One of Betteshanger's key picket locations was Brighton, at Shoreham power station, where scab coal was being unloaded.

The local Brighton paper, the Evening Argus (price 3p) carried a detailed news report that a miner from Kent, David Nash, was injured, run over by a scab lorry on a picket line at Southwick coal depot.

"Mr Nash was directing picketing while in constant contact with the miners strike committee HQ in Deal… Drivers of Lorries loaded with coal for hospitals or old-age pensioners were asked by the pickets to produce notes confirming where the coal was going. The pickets had talks with the crew of the ship James Rowan that had arrived at Shoreham harbour with coal for the power station at Shoreham. Central Electricity Generating Board workers refused to unload the shipment." (Evening Argus, 15th January 1972)

The organisation of legitimate deliveries of coal was done from within the very coal yard:

"We had an office in that coal yard, me and Barney Wynn – in their Board Room, we was agreeing with the Manager what deliveries could be made – only domestic and to hospitals, no industrial. We had a written agreement with them and then I done the same in Medway." (John Moyle, 15th January 1972)

The Brighton Evening Argus had further reports:

"A miner, his clothes filthy from nine hours of picketing, walked into a Shoreham washeteria last night and started undressing. Housewives gaped as they saw 28-year-old John Moyle stripped to his Paisley underpants. "This is how I work in the pits and I don't mind people seeing me like it." (Evening Argus, 17th January 1972)

John says that Betteshanger NUM should apply to Levis for copy write for their jeans advert, which showed a similar incident!

The Evening Argus also reported that day, that a miner had been on the back of a scab lorry which was carrying coal and not to the agreed pensioners and hospitals. He was throwing bags of coal off the back and calling to old people, "Do you want some coal?" The newspaper did not report this was the reason the miner was filthy and later needed the laundrette!

"As coal was thrown from the lorry an old lady called 'can you bring it round the back?'" (John Moyle, 2006)

But the Betteshanger miner was too busy dodging down alleys with the Police after him to take coal to pensioners' doors! On the same day a Coal lorry and it's scab driver were locked into the coal compound at Shoreham with the keys to the padlock being thrown into the River Adur. (Evening Argus, 17th January 1972)

Rank and file miners from Betteshanger went all over the country picketing:

"They was picketing and treated very well, all over supported by teachers and others and getting lots of money begging in London." (Dickie Prescott, 2006)

There was a lot of activity in the Medway towns and in Gravesend at paper mills, cement works and docks.

"This was our first real experience of organised picketing. The horrible picketing was at Gravesend; there was a big coal dump inside a Cement works. They hired thugs to drive the lorries, a driver and a mate; they put wire mesh over the windscreens and the mates had an iron bar. They got lorries lined up in convoy and the Police closed the road on each side, so the scabs could run straight out. We followed one down the M2 to the Rochester turn off; he got caught in traffic going up the hill. We jumped out the car and opened his tailboard; it was a big tipper and they were always overloaded. The vibrations shot the whole load (of coal) off; it closed the road." (John Moyle, 2006)

Some were arrested:

"I went to London. I got arrested at Neasden on a picket line. We was at this coal depot and I was arrested for giving out leaflets 'causing an obstruction' and the Prosecution said in court: 'Why were you standing on the footway giving out these leaflets?'

'Well I couldn't very well stand in the middle of the road could I?'

The court was in uproar and we were fined £30, which was a lot of money in those days. I also picketed at Battersea Power station with Barney Wynn, we stopped coal entering the power station with no problems. Anyway in 1972 we went everywhere, to the docks, to the universities, we spoke at meetings, they were very

Cartoon by Jimmy Brennan

Demonstration in Trafalgar Square

supportive. The Tory governments in the 1970s they never forgot the miners, we brought down the government." (Peter Holden, 2006)

Local newspapers report five Kent miners being fined in this incident, namely, M Rosser, L Smith, B Smith and H Tomas and Peter Holden.

Another area in which Kent and Betteshanger took a lead was in organising propaganda. Terry Harrison went to see the print workers' union:

"So I explained that my real mission was that we was going to have this demonstration in London and wanted something a bit more professional in the way of posters and things like that. Some cartoonist turned up from the national papers and I'd taken some drawings of Jimmy Brannan, who used to do a lot of our propaganda. I saw the drafts of these posters, they are good. You know 'Wanted. A living wage.' – that was the first poster that we had done. Then there was a picture of a miner and he carried a snap tin, lamp and God knows what with a capitalist in pinstripe trousers, – why are you carrying this one?

They asked, 'how many do you want?' and I'm thinking I am no authority or nothing, I have been trying to get a national leaflet out and, I have got the leaflet that I want producing, so he said something like, well we'll have quarter of a million!! 'We'll have a quarter of a million of the leaflet' and the leaflet turned out to be 'wanting a living wage', again and the back of it, although national, it was actually a copy of Kent. Kent's papers on the back of the national leaflet." (Terry Harrison, 2006)

The strike was not without its hardships. The Daily Mail reported on how Margaret Holden from Betteshanger village, wife of a striking miner:

" …has to make £5 do the work of £20." and "We've got to win and we're going to win."

The Evening News similarly reported miners' wives protest at the House of Commons at which Margaret expressed their determination to win. A canteen worker and miner's wife Isabel Rosser said:

"The mine workers have been black mailed into going back to work before when it has been said that the pits would be closed down. But it wont work this time. All the wives are determined not to let them go back until they get the money they deserve." (Evening News, February 1972)

The strike brought disparate groups together, including student supporters and other Trade Unionists and miners. Students produced a leaflet giving miners information on their social security entitlement for their dependents, ranging from £4.60 for an adult to £1.70 for an under five, plus rent and rates and free school meals. (Leaflet, National Archive) This leaflet, which I came across again in the National Archive in 2004, was actually run off on a duplicator in the basement of my house in Canterbury!

Nationally, the strike was accompanied by power cuts, the dramatic closure of the Saltley coke plant by pickets and the convening of the Wilberforce Enquiry into Miners' wages.

Jack Collins of Kent reported to the Wilberforce enquiry:

"Joe Dailey said 'Now let me get this straight, you are telling me that you brought a wage settlement in and some of your workers took a cut, a significant cut.' (Wilberforce Enquiry, 1972)

From left to right Terry Harrison and Jack Dunn

As the strike continued into February, the BBC reported that a state of emergency was declared and 2 days later, the three-day working week was introduced to save electricity. On the 19th February, after much negotiation, an agreement was reached between the National Executive Committee of the NUM and the Government. Picketing was called off and on the 25th February the miners accepted the offer in a ballot, returning to work on the 28th February.

The result of the strike was that the miners' wages became almost the highest amongst the working class. The strike also showed the country how important coal was to the economy.

Jack Dunn, Area General Secretary, wrote to unions who had been involved:

"Our members were overwhelmed at the kindness and friendship extended to them... It was a tremendous encouragement to us to see this tangible evidence of working class support; we won a magnificent victory through solidarity, perseverance and tenacity

– your assistance during this period was invaluable and we cannot thank you enough. It was a victory not only for the miners but for all those opposed to the present Tory government." (Whitfield Archive, 10th March 1972)

Anthony Barnett rather succinctly captured the mood:

"In the spring and summer of 1972, British Miners, Railwaymen and Dockers each in turn successfully defied the Heath Government. On no previous occasion in British history has the administration of the day suffered such a sequence of reverses from groups of workers pursuing economic demands. The results of these outstanding events took many socialists, at home and abroad, by surprise. That there would be hard struggles in 1972 was clear before the year began, that advances were possible was plain to see, but the scale of the victories which were actually won surpassed most expectation." (Anthony Barnett, New Left Review, January/February 1973)

In this victory Betteshanger played a key role.

1974 strike

During 1973 the wages of miners again began to slip and a national overtime ban had started on 12th November 1973.

The Welsh Miners Library reports that in February 1974 the miners' situation had deteriorated and a national miners strike was called again. The strike lasted four weeks. A state of emergency and a three-day working week were once again declared. The Prime Minister, Edward Heath, called a General Election hoping that the electorate would support the Government's attempts to deal with the deteriorating industrial situation, but the Conservative Party was defeated. The new Labour government reached a deal with the miners shortly afterwards.

The Betteshanger NUM Branch minutes report on an area conference of the 26th January 1974:

"…with a unanimous decision to 'call our members to vote for strike'

THE STRIKES OF 1972 AND 1974, AND OTHER ACTION

and 'Efforts to get 100% vote'. 'Our union must either fight to go forward or be left behind the wages earned by other unions'."

"Once again Kent was responsible for the London, Kent, Sussex areas and sent pickets to all parts required with very good effort."

During this dispute, newspaper headlines on 16th February 1974 read:

"Kent Miners Picket Deal Docks."

Picketing also took place at Didcot power station in Oxfordshire and Kent responded to that, ex-NUM members were students at Ruskin College in Oxford. The college takes union sponsored working class students onto pre-degree courses.

The Betteshanger NUM produced a leaflet:

"National Union of Mineworkers:

Strike Liaison Committee- Betteshanger Colliery Kent

We, the Liaison Committee, which is representative of all the workers who are on strike at Betteshanger colliery, want our fellow workers to understand our case.

The work of Britain's 287,000 mineworkers is hard and dangerous. Industrial accidents, pneumoconiosis (800 deaths in 1969) reap a heavy toll of life and limb. Everyone must agree, given the dangers to which the miner is exposed, that he is entitled to a fair wage, which pays regard to the dangers and hardships of his daily life.
...
The present basic rates of £19 per week underground, £18 per week surface, means a take home pay pf £14- £13 respectively, causing many of our members to be in a position of accepting welfare benefit. The offer, now withdrawn, of £2 for lower paid surface workers and £1.90 for lower paid underground workers is an insult.
...
British miners produce coal at approx. £6 per tone. By the time it is

75

handled by private distributors the price to the Housewife is £6 - £18 per ton

…

When the cost of living has risen by 11% in the last year, we are told to accept 7%. We know also that our rents will rise this year. We say, enough is enough. And we regret any inconvenience caused to our fellow workers.

We ask all workers and students for assistance in this dispute.
If the miners lose we all lose.

Strike Committee."

A national NUM area leaflet of the same time asks:

- DID YOU KNOW that a miner's real wage today is 5% <u>less</u> than in April 1972 after their last increase? Industrial companies profits were <u>up</u> by 42%.

The 1974 strike was settled by the result of the election. The answer to Heath's question, 'Who rules Britain?' was 'Not you!'

The Wilson Labour government settled the strike, in which Betteshanger, true to it's militant traditions, had played a leading role.

The Powder Dispute, and other disputes in the 1970s

Minutes of a meeting between the NUM and the NCB, (Whitfield Archive, 7th June 1974), report Joe Burke explaining that carrying the two canisters of (explosive) powder was a safety issue, because if men fell, both their hands were taken up. In addition, powder tins were left lying about in the headings with powder in them, in violation of health and safety law. The union had said that if nothing was done about this, each man using powder would carry only 5 lbs. of powder each. Mr Burke said that if they were to have a safe system at Betteshanger this incident with explosives must be cleared up and he was convinced that this would only be achieved by direct action.

Barney Wynne wrote to the Socialist Worker complaining that the 1974 national settlement was much more favorable to the Deputies and Overmen in that it had given them higher wage rises.

> "The outcome of this is a strong resentment among the NUM members. I work in an advanced heading, setting 14 foot steel arches. This involves the use of up to 50 or 60 pounds of powder, carried in heavy containers. By custom and practice this has been carried by the men on the job, but last week we refused to do this and this led to some of us walking out of the pit." (Socialist Worker, 6th April 1974)

But the militancy of the Betteshanger Branch did not always meet with favour from the National Executive, or regional officers of the NUM. There is correspondence to Branch secretaries in the NUM files at Whitfield concerning an incident in November 1974 when Branch members had agreed to march in the Lord Mayor's Parade in London. The NCB would pay travel expenses, subsistence and any loss of wages at standard rates for the Saturday. However, having had the Friday night 'with refreshments' out in London, Wes Chambers, the Betteshanger national delegate to the Executive rang Jack Dunn, of the Executive Committee, saying:

> "The lads are demanding that the normal payment at overtime rate should be paid for the Saturday."

Jack Dunn replied that they should take part in the parade and discuss the issue of payment afterwards, but they did not do so. Hobart House NCB office staff had to take their place.

A letter on the matter by Jack Dunn explained that the refusal to march was:
> "…a denigration of the Area Union and the National Union. It was agreed that a strong letter of complaint be sent to Branches on the whole matter and that Branches should investigate the matter and admonish those responsible for this unfortunate action." (Whitfield Archive, 1974)

The Branch took other actions during the 1970s, for example sending a bus of miners and the pipe band to a demonstration against the Pinochet regime in Chile.

They wrote to the NEC in July 1974 complaining that female NUM members in the canteen, and cleaners, were omitted from an award of a bonus in lieu of a weeks holiday.

The Branch proposed resolutions to annual conference in 1974 on:

- Equal Pay for Women
- Subsidies on mineworkers' rents
- Opposition to arms spending

The Branch also discussed issues such as excessive water in the cages and objected to the increase in officials in a supervisory capacity.

"This has grown out of all proportion, four to a face, one supervisor to three men." (NUM Branch minute, 1974)

They asked the NEC to examine the role of officials. The costs of their pensions, sick pay and so on, appeared:

"...out of all proportion to the contribution they make to the industry, NACODS (National Association of Colliery Overmen, Deputies and Shot firers) were refusing to appoint 'competent workmen' to operate in their absence." (NUM Branch minute, 1974)

Jack Dunn in the club

Deputies and Overmen would traditionally place the explosives and fire the shots to bring down coal. It had also been customary for the NACOD's members to allow a 'competent' NUM member to do so in their place. They were now refusing to do this.

In 1977, the Branch discussed the sale of pit houses and expressed concern that young members would not be able to find a home from the pit-housing list.

They also sent delegations to the picket line at Grunwick and described as deplorable:

> "The Police action by the Special Group in holding back pickets so that buses of scab workers could go to work in the union busting photographic firm in North London." (NUM Branch minutes, 1977)

I was present at Grunwick and after one incident I wrote a letter to a friend in which I spoke of seeing the Betteshanger banner dipping and waving in the crowd near the fiercest struggle at the factory gate.

An incorrect suggestion was made in the Morning Star (the Communist Party paper) that a Betteshanger miner had pushed Arthur Scargill at Grunwicks, leading to the latter's arrest for being in the road. A photo appeared in the Morning Star with the possible culprit's face ringed. The caption read, "Who is this man?"; the man was John Moyle. Jack Dunn, (a member of the Communist Party) later apologised for this.

Grunwick strikers, with Jack Dromey and Patricia Hewitt came down to Kent to make a presentation to Jack Dunn of a painting expressing their thanks. This painting still hangs in the office at Magness House. The whole affair shows more evidence of Betteshanger, and the Kent area's involvement in the national class struggle of the 1970s and 80s.

The very heritage of Betteshanger was revealed in their prominent role in the 1972 and 1974 strikes, as well as other political struggles of the 1970s.

SIXTY YEARS OF STRUGGLE

THE 1980s AND THE 1984 NATIONAL STRIKE

7

Threat to Snowdown in 1981

The major issue for Betteshanger Branch, at the beginning of the 1980s, was the threatened closure of the Kent pit Snowdown. The area NUM Council meeting on the 13th February 1981 noted:

> "The NCB area Director reported upon his recommendation to close Snowdown colliery before the end of June 1981 and above 450 men would be transferred to the remaining two Kent collieries."

To which the area NUM Secretary said that the NCB Director was:

> "Acting like a feudal baron, deciding who would eat and who will not, and that he was acting as an agent of the Tory Government, putting men on the dole." (Jack Collins)

The Area Council therefore called for an overtime ban in all the pits with an agreement to strike.

This threat to Snowdown had an overwhelming impact on all the Kent pits at a time when the Betteshanger Chairman, John Moyle, held the area Presidency.

The following resolution was passed at Betteshanger Branch General Meeting on Sunday 5th July 1981:

> "We re-affirm Branch policy on redundancy and support development of Snowdown No. 9 Seam with adequate safeguards for continuation of all three Kent pits with manpower at minimum of 3,000."

Jack Collins was reported in the Dover Express, 20th February 1981, saying that the transfer of men from Snowdown would put the other pits in an unviable position, having a burden of having to produce an extra 2,000 tonnes a week.

A taped interview at the South Wales Miners Library in Swansea, with John Moyle and Jack Collins, explains the position and the Union's case for a lower seam at Snowdown, with a new drivage. The board wouldn't, at first, accept it:

> "They said we must accept 300 job losses – redundancies. They put out rumours to get at the older, sick miners saying, 'We're doing you a favour.' "

> We had a difficulty with older miners because we stopped all redundancies.

> The Board said we can have the capital investment but only if we accept the redundancies! Of course, we want the capital investment without the redundancies!"
> (John Moyle, Area President, Swansea tape)

All the unions NACODS, BACUM, APEX, etc., were on a joint Union platform at Margate, attended by 3000 men. They announced that they were committed to undertake action to maintain Snowdon:

> "They couldn't split the Unions. They managed to split us on redundancy. They wanted 300 jobs out of the area. They've said to the other unions, you can pick what men you want and we'll replace them by NUM members.

> We stopped men transferring from the NUM to other Unions." (John Moyle, Swansea tape)

The NUM position was that there should be improved early retirement and retirement on the grounds of ill health, but that the jobs should not be made redundant:

Arnold Moyle and John Moyle with 100 year old miner. 1983

"You cannot award anyone enough redundancy, men are being put on the dole for life, because there is no other work. Every man that takes a redundancy is denying another man a job." (Jack Collins, Dover Express, 20th February 1981)

"At Betteshanger they said do you want another 100 men? But we're saying we're not having men at the expense of Snowdon." (John Moyle, Swansea tape)

There was a three-day strike in February 1981:

"Graham Brett, a member of the (strike) committee formed at Betteshanger, told the Dover Express, 'We are going to tell the Department of Energy that we are not doing to sacrifice any pits or our jobs.'" (Dover Express, 20th February 1981)

"After the strike they accepted our case. We said we'd be prepared to ask for 80 volunteers to go to Tilmanstone for 2 years, while

Snowdon develops the lower seams and then they can go back. The Coal Board was now prepared to talk about retaining 700 men at Snowdon." (Jack Collins, Swansea tape)

"It was you and I, Jack that exposed their running down of Snowdon. The manager said I'm not having Johnny Moyle telling me how to run my pit! Three weeks later he ran out of the back door, left the job, and the other managers didn't even know £2 million of power supports were left in pit, and they talk about losses!" (John Moyle, Swansea tape)

There were those who disagreed with the tactic in this dispute, feeling that refusing the redundancies lost the NUM support. But, after only a few days strike, the NCB changed its mind. With the victory, which kept Snowdown open, life at Betteshanger continued as usual with the occasional dispute.

Pickets round a brazier

Life as normal

Management continue to take strong action, for example on 26th September 1983 they wrote to '24s' team about their:

"...riding the pit at 6.30pm ...this irresponsible attitude to your work cannot be allowed to continue, so the practice of doubling back onto Friday afternoon when on night shift is stopped". (J R Wells, letter in archive at Wingfield Dover)

'Riding the pit' meant leaving the pit, while 'doubling back' was a practice whereby the Friday night shift could decide instead to work on afternoons.

In another incident, discussed in a meeting with the Board on 3rd October 1983, the Shift Charge Engineer had instructed a man to stop working on Air Doors in Number 2 Pit bottom and go to attend a supposed emergency on the South East pump. The man disputed that this was an emergency and was sent out of the pit. The Shift Charge Engineer did not deploy anyone else to go to the 'Emergency' but rode out of the pit at the same time. The branch NUM Chairman said:

"They were opposed to a man being sent out of the pit purely on a question of redeployment. Sending men out should be for violence, breaches of the Act involving danger to themselves and others etc." (Board Minutes of meeting, 3rd October 1983)

The 1984 Strike

The 1984 strike is a key marker in British and European labour history. The countrywide story is well known. As for Betteshanger, protest and action was part of the fabric of life. Betteshanger was amongst the first to strike in March 1984, following the threat to close Cortonwood

A brief chronology shows how events unfolded:

"Betteshanger & the National Strike 1984/1985

March 1984	Branch meeting at Deal Welfare endorses strike in support of Yorkshire, following threat to close Cortonwood. Pickets (from Kent) in Warwickshire and Leicestershire. Deal Women's Support Group formed.
April 1984	Police stop cars at Dartford tunnel, threaten arrest as soon as cars leave Kent. Arrests in Colchester. March from Kent to Nottingham lead by Terry French and Jack Dunn. McGibbons and Smart (strike breakers) turn up for work.

May	1984	Kent wives sit in at DHSS offices; arrests at S African embassy for Dumping Coal. Arrests for sitting on railway line. Betteshanger occupied. Scabs sign agreement not to return and Management agree that pit is safe and stable. March and rally in London. Death of Dave Jones, miner. Branch Committee and others sacked.
July	1984	Notts children have holiday with Kent miner's families. More arrests in Colchester.
Aug	1984	Dutch convoy of food impounded at Dover docks.
Sept	1984	Police and 6 scabs at work on tip at Betteshanger.
Oct	1984	Food convoy from French CGT.
Nov	1984	Meeting in Granville theatre Arthur Scargill speaks.
Dec	1984	Jury fails to reach verdict re Tazey and French. More arrests. SERTUC (South East Region TUC) provides Turkeys and Xmas puddings for all strikers.
Jan	1985	Tazey and French found guilty given 3 and 5 years in prison. Kent miners arrested at House of Lords; John Moyle addresses House.
Feb	1985	Deal women's support march from Sandwich to Richborough. Garden of England play about Betteshanger.
March	1985	Delegate conference votes 98:91 for return, with no amnesty for sacked men.

The march to Nottingham

Kent rejects the return and sends pickets to S Wales and Yorkshire before finally recommending return.

1985 and on.   Victimised remain without justice."
(Tommy Early's pamphlet)

During the strike the Kent area produced a leaflet, summarising the arguments of the Oxford Economist, Andrew Glyn. (A Glyn. The case against pit closure, 5th October 1985)

The leaflet highlighted some economic home truths:

" 'Closing uneconomic pits means higher taxes and lower living standards'

- Cost of dispute is £5 per working person a week
- Cost of redundancies is double what would cost to keep pits open
- Coal Board give CEGB £1.5m subsidy
- Coal Board sells coal at 40% below cost of oil
- Cost of dispute £405m in lost wages and pension contribution of miners. £27.5m loss to NCB.
- Lost Tax Revenue £300m and extra Policing £125m
- £91,024 per miner redundant double the subsidies to keep miners in work"

Paying out pickets in the strike

There were, however, a small minority at Betteshanger who opposed the National Strike.

"We knew that a strike was coming and it was just my personal opinion, we had a justified case, but I didn't think a total strike was the answer because they (the Government and Coal Board) were prepared for it. There was 2 year's coal in the country. There was a ballot at the Club in Cowdray Square and a show of hands. Great fighting speeches were made: Terry Harrison, Johnny Moyle. There were about 20 of us put our hands up against the strike." (Dickie Prescott, 2006)

Picketing in 1984 and the Womens' Support Group

The Women's Support Committee Betteshanger, as throughout the coalfields, were crucial to the community and the dispute:

"They set up a Kent Women's Committee to organise things, that was with Kay Sutcliffe (at Snowdown) and Margaret Holmes and we went to the National meetings. They had a meeting once a week – Dover, Aylesham, Tilmanstone – the other pits- the women all got together.

At first, with Janet Dunn and Margaret Holden they went to Magness House, strike Headquarters and began making pots of tea. They then asked the women to set up a soup kitchen, but to set this up they needed money.

We were fund raising, making sure everyone was fed; had food parcels; we organised children's holidays and coach trips."
(Liz French, 2006)

"We were in the cottage next to Magness House; all the food came down from London from the Daily Mirror printers and all the families got parcels every week – tea, coffee, butter, tins, sugar – everything to make a meal. Some people were nasty, would look at a parcel and say 'is that all you've got?' There was also a meal served up at the club lunchtime. This went on for about a year until the strike finished.

Liz French

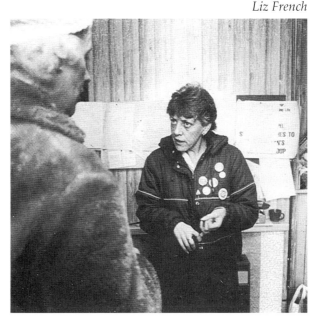

Turkeys came from Smithfields; they were so big they couldn't get into the oven! Some of the women took children on holiday to Denmark. We used to go to concerts in

London during the strike; men were away for weeks begging and bringing money back. The community is closer now; you got to know people who came for their food." (Sheila Shooter, 2006)

But money for food and support did not arrive of its own accord:

"So some women went and stood on platforms asking for money, telling our cause...I went to every nook and cranny in London: Brixton, Kensington, Southwark. I went to Brighton, Oxford, and so many places. We were always speaking to the converted. Then I went abroad to Belgium, Germany, all over. We even went to the USA, standing on a lorry near the White House; they called us Communists. The most frightening thing was I had never been anywhere on my own, had never even been on a train on my own and there I was going to Germany on my own!" (Liz French, 2006)

Meals served in the club

The Branch Minutes reported on the women's' activities:

"The womens' support group had by now increased its membership of women who would travel to speak. Parcels and support were coming from Germany. Kent had one delegate on the National Women Against Pit Closures Committee, which were 75% miner's wives. There were to be whole range of Christmas activities and turkeys were expected from the Print Workers Union." (NUM minutes, December 1984)

"The girls had a permanent stew pot and they made breakfasts, bacon & egg, whatever there was, meals for 2,000. That Christmas I never slept for 24 hours, making sure everyone had a turkey, a pudding and all the children had a toy." (Liz French, 2006)

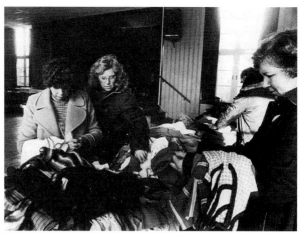

Women sorting clothes

"Food/clothes were piling in from everywhere from the Continent; the Women's Support Group organised the distribution." (Terry Birkett, 2006)

There was even a play about the strike called 'Garden of England'. Written and performed by the 7:84 Theatre Company, it was based on Liz French and the Betteshanger experience. Liz French is still friendly today with the actress who played her.

"We staged 'The Garden of England', a tribute to the heroic struggle of the miners' wives." (7:84 Theatre Company web site)

Liz carried on campaigning, speaking, and going on the road for the sacked miners. Her conclusion, looking back on the 1984/85 strike was:

"We loved it; everyone was like a community, everyone helped each other. We were all skint, all in debt, but we were together. If it hadn't been for the strike I'd never have gone to America, never had met all those people". (2006)

The struggle of the oppressed has no national boundaries

International Support

Supporters of the National Strike came from across Europe. They would visit Deal, as it was very near their arrival at the Dover Docks. Many nationalities were represented. They came from Belgium, France, Holland, Denmark, Germany and Russia.

"The Belgians, the Russians were marvellous – our international links were so helpful". (Terry Burkett, 2006)

The Danish delegation was recommended a demonstration outside the British Embassy in Copenhagen and presented the Betteshanger Branch a collection of £6,000!

International supporters wrote saying, " ...all felt that the future of their jobs and Union Movement rested on the successful outcome of the Miners' Strike." (Branch Minutes, 1984)

During the strike Jack Collins asked John Moyle to accompany him to a function at the Russian Embassy. As John Moyle recounted, they approached the Polish Ambassadors, who spoke English, and Jack made an inquiry:

"What about this coal from Poland that is being imported into Britain?"

The Ambassador explained,

> "Oh, we support the British miners; we make collections for them and so on. But we have contracts we have to honour with British Companies."

Jack replied firmly, with a stabbing finger:

> "'The only contracts you have to honour, comrade is with the British Working Class!' Everyone had red faces and tried to pretend it hadn't happened." (John Moyle interview, 2006)

Arthur Scargill mentioned, in his interview with me in 2007, that he was involved in a similar encounter.

Sequestration

The funds of the National Union were taken over, or 'sequestrated', by the courts on behalf of the Thatcher Government.

The appointment of Sequestrators and a Receiver was unprecedented in British Law. A special national conference in December had instructed the Union Officers not to give any help to the sequestrators.

The Branch Minutes reported that the:

> "Sequestration of NUM funds was taking place, following the refusal of the Union to purge its contempt." (28th October 1984)

The Branch commented:

> "NEC report indicates that the Coal Board were not free agents and McGregor was controlled by the Cabinet. People asked what had happened to the TUC Guidelines and why lorry drivers were still crossing picket lines." (NUM minutes, 3rd September 1984)

In January 1985, the Branch reported a demonstration at Tilbury.

Team chopping wood

"This could be a further tie-hold to power workers to keep them to the TUC guidelines, which recommended not crossing picket lines".

As Liz French explains:

"We needed more than the money from collections; we had to stop the power, the print, the trains. We couldn't win on our own. It was a tragedy we didn't get the support." (2006)

Keeping warm, keeping going

As with the 1942 strike, keeping warm was a big issue. Deal miners' homes were heated with coal, but sometimes while away on the picket lines, other forms of heat were used. Indeed a picket reported to me that he had never been as cold in his life as when away picketing, where the person's whole house was heated by a one-bar electric fire!

There was a long debate over the delivery of coal to retired people, who normally had free coal. It must be remembered that retired miners', and working miners', houses in Deal were still entirely heated by coal and there was no money for electricity bills, The problem was that the Board were saying that the only coal available to deliver to pensioners was from scab working pits, like Coventry.

The Branch committee took the view that no scab coal would be handled and that the Union would look at hardship cases. The Branch spent £3,500 of strike money in keeping old people warm.

The issue of keeping people warm was of supreme importance. A logging team was set up and some farmers allowed miners to chop down trees. Wood was brought to the yard of Magness House and bagged up for delivery to pensioners and others.

"We used to mend all the pickets' cars for free." (John Moyle, 2006)

Later after the strike two lads (ex-miners) opened a garage and ran it successfully for fifteen years. They also used to cut each other's hair and help each other in many ways.

All these activities, logging, collecting and distributing food, repairing cars, were a crucial part of the strike, helping to keep morale up in difficult times.

Arrests and Prisoners

A large number of Betteshanger miners were arrested during the strike. OH Parsons Solicitors dealt with their cases. Some of these arrests occurred at the beginning of the strike and some incidents were televised.

Picket line

Footage was also included in a television play about the strike, shown in 2006. One lad was even arrested while giving first aid at the side of the road.

Letters from OH Parsons Solicitors' to the Betteshanger Branch, held in the Magness House office files, shed some light on a couple of incidents:

"Mark Best was arrested during the occupation of Hobard House (NCB Headquarters in London) – at the time he was trying to assist James Waddell who was trying to climb into the window on a rope – the rope was caught on James Waddell's finger and was causing him a lot of pain – he cried for help and Mark went to assist him. As he did so, a Police Constable who was no doubt practising for the Police Olympics, threw himself at Mark and brought him to the ground. Your member was later charged with obstructing a Police Officer in the execution of his duty. The case was dismissed.

Your members, L Sweeting, K Morris, D. Cable and T. Cable were charged with using insulting words and behaviour following an incident when a bag of coal was dropped at the gates of the South African Embassy on the 1st June"

They were charged with action contrary to Litter Act."

John Moyle recollects the injustice:

"I was arrested for being in the wrong place at the wrong time, and there was jumped up charges – assault on scabs, on pigs. I wasn't any different to anyone, we were all arrested. I used to escape over the back garden fence; but the best thing over the back there, the women's son was a pig! (Policeman) I used to escape into the Miner's Welfare, and they never came in there. The would never come in there for yer – that was off limits for them." (John Moyle, 2006)

An older miner remembered the damage caused by Police action:

"In 1984 they allowed Police to go in and gave them a rough do. It split families; some still won't speak to relatives who were in the Police. The Police were terrible." (Charles Grant, 2006)

Some arrested miners wrote to the NUM Branch from Prison:

"In replying to this letter, please write on the envelope

Number 67894   Name:
                       HM Prison
                       Longport
                       Canterbury
                       Kent

Brian and all the girls and lads back home.

The Canterbury Eight would like to thank you for your support, during our unforeseen holiday. Thank you all for keeping a supply of food, beer, tobacco and also the radio's.

This thank you also includes the girls in the kitchen at the Welfare Club and also everybody that's keeping our visits going.

We also extend our thanks to all the lads on the picket line, the lads in Magness House and also the girls in 'The Cottage'.

Our visit here was unexpected but quite pleasant, this was made possible by the great support, which has come from a great community, which we are pleased to be part of.

'I would rather be a picket than a scab'.

PS: At last Terry Birkett knows where we are.

Signed by 8 prisoners…"

There was a Ballot for 50p a week levy of members to support families, and sacked and imprisoned members. Members were also invited to write to them in prison.

The Arrest and trials of Terry French

Other arrests concerned the attempt to prevent the return of scabs to the pit.

> "Three policemen gave evidence to the effect that a red Morris Marina motorcar had drawn into the entrance to the colliery following another car. The first car stopped, surrounded by pickets. The police formed two lines to keep pickets away from the cars. The first car pulled away but for some reason the red Morris Marina was stopped with its near side front wheel on the kerb. As it was about to draw away Mr. Todd went to the front of the car and held it by the grill thus preventing it from moving off. He then sat on the bonnet. Two of the policemen who gave evidence then said they took him from the bonnet and moved him some distance to the rear of the picket lines! He was found not guilty.

> Mr. French is said to have 'broken through' the police line, jumped on to the front of the car, grabbed hold of the roof rack, and then stayed on the bonnet of the car, bashing the window and shouting 'Bastard Scab'. The police account was that the car then continued travelling at a speed of between 5 and 10 mph for a distance, which varied in police accounts from 20 yards to 40 yards. The car then stopped and Mr French fell off the front. He was then picked up and arrested and cautioned for using threatening language." (OH Parsons letter, 1984)

> "Terry was arrested 15 times for various things on picket lines. The main one was at Wivenhoe where he was charged with damaging a Policeman. This copper came over a 6ft fence, supposedly Terry beat him up, and then he (copper) climbed back over again with a dislocated shoulder.

> At first there was a hung Jury but by the second trial there were 22 coppers to say he'd beaten one up. He was eventually found Guilty and got 5 years (Chris Tazey got 3) He was in Maidstone, Wandsworth, North Eye, and Ford Prisons. By the end they were

shipping him everywhere. He served two years and three months. He was also a sacked miner!" (Liz French, 2006)

Betteshanger Branch records reveal that Terry French and Chris Tazey sent messages from prison urging the community to: "Keep fighting to victory."

The police often arrested but didn't press charges. They placed Bind-overs requiring people not to visit pits or picket lines, this kept people off picket lines. The Branch Committee recommended that people arrested at Colchester to not accept Bind-overs, as the Police would find it hard to make the charges stick.

Police Charge Sheet.

ESSEX POLICE
COPY FOR ACCUSED PERSON

Person charged.

Surname.

Christian Names.

Address.

Place and date of birth/Occupation.

You are charged with the following offence(s):

At Wivenhoe in the County of Essex on 18th April 1984, in a certain public place called West Street did use threatening, abusive and/or insulting words and/or behaviour with intent to provoke a Breach of the Peace or whereby a Breach of the Peace was likely to be occasioned.

CONTRARY TO: Section 5 Public Order Act 1936
                   Section 7 Race Relations Act 1965

Civil Liberties

On a national level during the strike, some of the most significant erosions of civil liberties concerned the Police blockades of the Dartford Tunnel. This was intended to prevent Kent miners leaving the county to picket in other parts of the country.

OH Parsons solicitors commented:

> "The Dartford Tunnel Injunction case in March last year, when we failed to obtain an injunction against the Chief Constable of Kent, for the undoubtedly illegal action on his officers' part in stopping your members going through the Tunnel on their way to picket in the Midlands and the North." (OH Parsons, 1985)

Just prior to the occupation of the pit, John Moyle, speaking in London, stopped the night at my Hackney house. He explained that when the Police stopped his car, at the Dartford tunnel and elsewhere, he kept a tape recorder on the seat and switched it on to record the conversation.

On leaving the house in the morning John Moyle found that his car, parked five doors away, had been broken into. His golf clubs and tennis racket had been ignored, but his brief case was gone. Later that day there was a knock on the door of the Hackney house. The poet John Hegley, who was also living there, answered. A Policeman handed in 'Mr Moyle's briefcase'. Neither the theft, nor the address at which he was staying, had been reported to the police. They somehow knew where and when to look for Mr. Moyle, either from phone tapping or surveillance. Inside the briefcase the papers (no doubt duly copied) were all in order, but the tape recorder and tape were missing.

Police surveillance and action was not an uncommon event for activists in the 1980's.

Mc Gibbon, professional strike-breaker

Mr. McGibbon had arrived at Betteshanger to work, coming from the Cowley British Leyland car plant. In Cowley, he and his wife had been at the forefront of activity aimed at destabilising the militant Trade Union leadership of Alan Thornett in the mid 1970s. This included Mrs. McGibbon leading a 'wives' anti-striking movement. In Cowley, I witnessed Mrs. McGibbon holding an anti-strike meeting in Oxford town hall. Striking car workers wives and other women, including myself, protested during the meeting.

It seemed curious that the McGibbons should wish to come to another militant area?

> "Why did this man with no previous experience of coal-mining travel from Oxfordshire, all the way to Kent to start work in his 40's in a coal mine? It was extremely unusual for any man unused to mining, or not from a mining area or tradition, to start work in a mine at that age. There is only one explanation McGibbon, as he had done in Cowley, was playing a deliberate role to sabotage the strike.
>
> In June we got knowledge of people going back to work. McGibbon, he was financed by National Association for Freedom, Mrs. McGibbon had made a speech to the Conservative Conference; Aims of Industry set him up in a boarding house in Ramsgate." (Terry Harrison, 2006)

Before the strike Terry Birkett had found McGibbon in a compromised position.

> "I found him asleep down the pit – a sackable offence.
> He led a party of 20 people trying to break the strike, some for marital reasons; some didn't agree with the strike, some were under debt.
> In 1984 we'd no sooner gone into strike than Alan Thornett (Union deputy convenor at British Leyland Oxford) sent me paper cuttings from Oxford about McGibbons and his wife. I couldn't believe it,

this bloke had come here as an ordinary bloke. The only problem we had with him was his team had come in: the Puffler and the Monkey Puff, they complained bitterly about this lazy sod they had on the face, they wanted him removed and, to my shame, I asked them to give him a second chance!" (Terry Harrison, 2006)

As Peter Holden explains:

"As the year went by, the steelworkers, the newspapers, the teachers, were all involved with the government. They were trying to break the working class and the first time we knew it was when we were infiltrated by scabs. McGibbons and co. if the mines were open now, we'd soon be asking if anyone came here, especially at that age, we'd ask, 'Where were you before; were you involved in any problems?' We'd have found out that he was anti union." (Peter Holden, 2006)

McGibbon had gone back to work on the 16th April 1984 and was at the forefront of the return to work movement.

"We couldn't believe we had this celebrity, it was infiltration by the National Association of Freedom. I couldn't believe it and there was also talk about the CIA involvement. But the sad thing was that they did carry some of our members with them, some who weren't very bright, Benny from Crossroads types; they'd been provided a job at the Union's behest. So we were surprised when they went along with him." (Terry Birkett, 2006)

Occupation of Betteshanger

In the summer of 1984, for the second time, Betteshanger was occupied. And once more, not for wages, but for jobs. In 1960 the occupation was against redundancies, in 1984 it was to save the pit. The managers were saying, it was dangerous, there was gas and it would have to close. The causes of the stay down were two fold, one to test these assertions of management that the pit was now unsafe and two, to prevent the scab McGibbon working.

"McGibbon was going to start on the Monday, so we went down the pit on the Sunday night. Management used to go to inspect the shaft; so all the winding gear was in order. One of our members, a winder, wound us down, we sat our stall out, and we visited the place where management said it was deteriorating. It was a pack of lies. I stayed down twice – in 1960 and 1984." (Terry Birkett, 2006)

During the second stay down in 1984 it was decided that Terry B would be 'better use' on the surface as an organiser, so he returned to Magness House to lead things from there.

Bob Nichols kept a detailed diary on this stay down.

Extracts from the diary read:

"Day One – Sunday 17th June 1984

The 8 lads met in the carpark on pit top at 14.55. Waited for NUM Winder to arrive. At 15.00 hours another group of lads took over the control room. We then made our way to number two-pit bank.

There was nobody else down the pit when we arrived at 19.00 hours. All we were equipped with was a lamp each, a self-rescuer and one safety lamp. We then started to get organised for a long stay i.e.: stretcher (beds) and offices for accommodation. Two hours later we received our first supplies – water, sandwiches, chewing tobacco, sweets, and packs of cards.

Day Two – Monday 18th June 1984

We woke at 03.30 and split into four groups of two over the pit to inspect all faces and main roadways. All teams had returned by 06.30 and reported that the districts they had inspected were in very good condition. Six members of Nacods arrived at 19.00 hours for their daily inspection of the mine, and also brought down on the same cage our breakfast – urn of tea, sandwiches, roast pots and more chewing tobacco. We then made a shower out of an old fire bucket with a water bagging and a wooden platform to stand on.

John and Alan then made a cricket bat and ball and set up a pitch. This was hardly the Oval – seven men in pit boots, underpants, and a hand made wooden bat, cloth ball and tin sheet as wickets in a dimly lit roadway.

13.00 hours, Mel had to leave us so he could see a specialist about his knee, so he rode the mine with the NACOD members who had finished their shift. On the cage that rode against them was our first hot meal – sausages and chips.

It was decided that Terry Burkett would be put to better use on the surface as an organiser. So after we had our second hot meal of the day – fish and chips, Terry rode the mine. The rest of the lads made phone calls to their wives and children. Our spirits were high when we turned in at 10.00pm.

Day Three – Tuesday 19th June 1984

We woke at 06.00hours to a phone call from the lads on the surface telling us of the Police presence to assist the two scabs to lean on a shovel a mile away down the tip. We then cleaned our accommodation and did some washing i.e.: socks, pants and T-shirts. We then had to spend the rest of the day in just our footwear. This proved to be awkward, so spent some time making a pair of sandals out of some belting. Mid-morning we heard that the Board were seeking a High Court Injunction against us so we quickly made arrangements with the lads on top to get as much supplies down as quickly as possible.

One hour later a well-stocked cage arrive, about 5-7 days supplies.

15.00 hours we were in contact with the lads on top who had just told us that they had sent the Bailiff and the Under Manager – away with a barrage of water canons as they tried to serve the summons on the lads. We decided that we have to take certain precautions against them trying to remove us from underground. So we chained all the gantries up so nobody could deck without us assisting them. We then made a few phone calls to our families to tell them not to worry about what they might hear on the news etc. because we were in total control, and although we hoped they would we did not think that the pigs would try to come and get us out. For the rest of the day we were in constant contact with the lads up top who also put the phone near the TV every time the news came on so we could be up-to-date with our dispute.

At 18.30 hours the lads sent a TV cameraman down to see us and also some more supplies.

Although this might have been our last lot of supplies, the lads were still more determined than ever that until the Board retract their statement and announce publicly that the pit is in good order and gas free, also that the Police leave the Coal Board property, we were not ready to talk.

We came to the decision that if we got some kind of statement from the Board that this pit was in good order, and gas free, we would then end our dispute.

Day Four – Wednesday 20ᵗʰ June 1984

This was a very tense and anxious few hours for us, as we could sense victory – but we had to make sure it was good, hard, and concrete with no sell-outs.

09.30 hours, John told us that the Board were prepared to make a statement saying that our pit was in good condition and gas free. After hearing this, we decided that it was time to call off the demonstration and return to the surface.

We then decided to have a final game of cricket and try to take some of our emotional feelings out of the situation.

As the cage started to move up, we knew it was nearly all over and we had a great victory under our belts.

We then went through the air doors, to the most emotional reception anyone could wish for. The first to greet us was our wives, who were the backbone of our stay down the mine. We then went to the lamp room and the offices to ask the lads to de-occupy the premises. They all came out and we congratulated them on one hell of a job they had done, because they were the heroes that were under intense pressure, but they still made sure that we were safe and looked after underground.

Total hours underground – sixty-eight.

VICTORY TO THE MINERS

Bob Nicholls
Wednesday 20ᵗʰ June 1984"

Peter Holden brilliantly described the situation on the surface:

"So one particular day, in the Welfare, 2/3 miners approached me saying, 'Peter, we're going to occupy the mine, will you come with us?'

Our aim was to get the management to sign a statement saying the mine was workable and safe. So I took the main offices over; we went in there; we knocked on the door and the under manager came and said, 'Can I help you?' And we said, 'We've come to occupy the mine!'
'I beg your pardon?'
'From now on we've occupied the mine and will you leave?'

So they all left, as simple as that. We got the forklift from the yard and put cement bags behind each door, a four-foot barrier so no one could get in. They sent about 3000 police down here; the local police would have nothing to do with it, they had to live with us afterwards; so they sent the Met. I think the Inspector approached Terry Harrison and Terry said, 'There are some very angry men here, I shouldn't come in here.'

Because of the threat, we had drums of oil on the tops of stairs, we had ball bearings, and we had water in case of gas coming in. We had hosepipes; it was serious stuff. This is why Terry convinced the officers they couldn't take us by force. I went up onto the water tower and sat up they're for two nights; it was summer time; I could see all the police up there on the top road. There were vans and there were police walking up and down. We used to send people out onto the marshes and I could see police running after them, but we knew our way around the marshes and we were jumping dykes and the police were running after and jumping and falling in the water. It was great fun, but serious.

It wasn't just police they had there, there was armed forces. The way they were marching up and down, it was precision marching, the police don't do that and they had no numbers on their shoulders." (Peter Holden, 2006)

During the occupation Terry Harrison, on behalf of the Branch, negotiated an agreement signed by McGibbon (the handwritten agreement is in the Branch Archive at Dover). It states that he would not continue working during the strike. This was one of the terms of the ending of the occupation. After the occupation ended McGibbon broke the agreement and returned to work.

Sackings

After the stay down, the occupiers and NUM Branch Committee were all sacked. Thirty-four men, including some people who had not even been involved with the occupation:

"The NCB were obdurate and vicious over the Betteshanger men, and I remember 2/3 they sacked, people who were never even in the occupation. One of them, Peter Fullbrook, the only time he went there during the occupation was to take me there in his car to a meeting and he was sacked. His life collapsed from then, he was suicidal, drank, his marriage broke up and he died a young death". (Terry Harrison, 2006)

In 1985, following the end of the strike, McGibbon and others took Court Proceedings against the Union Branch and against sacked miners. He claimed that scab mines had been physically intimidated following their return to work. McGibbon requested the Court:

> "To order that the Defendants be restrained from entering the colliery premises".

It was on this basis that injunctions were placed against the Branch Committee.

The Branch received reports of the threats made to striking miners and their families which did not 'warrant lurid press and media reporting', referring to the large press coverage on what happened to scabs.

> "Injunctions were taken against men who were sacked at Betteshanger. The employers went to Court and took injunctions stopping any of these men they'd dismissed going on Coal Board property <u>ever.</u> Full stop! The reasons they gave they didn't need a reason, you was a coalminer and that was it and in the eyes of the Union it was a waste of time defending it; they didn't have any money anyway. We were begging on the removal of injunctions, we had difficulty getting the Union to support the removal after the strike. The Union said they hadn't the money to go to Court, even though it wouldn't be a horrendous amount of money and wouldn't be too difficult, because the strike was over. Although there were certain people they were determined wouldn't ever return. At Betteshanger they dismissed 85-90% of the branch officials, all the officials who were committed Chair, Treasurer, Secretary, all the committee." (John Moyle, 2006)

There were disagreements as to whether other men should be co-opted onto the Branch Committee to replace those sacked and represent the men in the pit. (See next chapter)

End of the Strike

By February 1985 the branch was reporting that there was some pressure coming from Wales and elsewhere for talks to settle the dispute.

The Chairman and Secretary urged people not to spread rumours and to recognise that the 'media were attempting to *once* again set up a return to work movement'.

"There was no agreement on a return, the strike really collapsed. Most miners went back 'Heads held high' and bands playing. But because there was no agreement the sacked stayed sacked. So when Kent met, they decided they weren't going to go along with the return. We decided to stay out and send pickets again to the other areas. I suppose it was a weakness, that we weren't big enough to recognise that the strike was lost". (Terry Harrison, 2006)

Terry Harrison the Secretary said at the Branch meeting before the return:

"On behalf of the members dismissed, we wish those returning to work, a safe and accident free future." (17th March 1985)

It was difficult for the men when they went back to work.

"When we got down the pit they knew we was defeated. So they (Deputies) started, 'You'll do this, you'll do that', but they didn't realise, blokes would do half a shift and then say, 'sod you', 'I'm going home'. The Managers never understood that if you got half a shift in you, you had more money than you'd had all year! They could go on strike 2-3 times a week and still have more than they'd had. The officials didn't understand and were still being dogmatic, but the men said 'no, we're not going to be kicked around." (Dickie Prescott, 2006)

By the time of the return, the Branch meeting gave unanimously a Vote of Confidence in the entire committee for its work in the strike.
The Chairman spoke on behalf of all members saying:

"We could not claim a victory. We had to go on to the further challenges that confront miners: The campaign to reinstate men dismissed for carrying out Trade Union rights and duties. The campaign to get miners out of prison, they were political prisoners. The miners of Betteshanger and their wives were the finest people in the British Coalfields. We should also remember those who had given their lives, those injured." (Branch minutes, 10th February 1985)

The Branch recorded that the interests of the sacked and the political prisoners were uppermost in their minds.

Conclusion

"The strike had not been about wages, better conditions or any material gain.

It had been waged on principle; the principle that miners' jobs were held by each generation of workers in trust for those who would come after them, and must not be wantonly destroyed." (NUM web site, 2006)

In Betteshanger, that principle had been clearly upheld and was to be so for the next four years until closure.

BETTESHANGER COLLIERY: THE LAST YEARS 1985 TO 1989 8

With 80% of the Branch Committee sacked, the last years were initially characterised by the battle on behalf of the victimised and to maintain wages and conditions. Betteshanger was the only pit in the country where, of the 34 sacked miners, none were reinstated. Only 333 nationwide suffered this fate. Therefore, in the whole country, the sacked men at Betteshanger represented 10% of those who were not reinstated. On March 13th 1986, the East Kent Mercury reported a 24-hour stoppage in protest about the sacked colleagues.

The injunctions against the Branch Committee meant that sacked officers of the Union could not visit the pit.

"We were elected officials who have got to report to the workforce. So it was to the advantage of employers to keep these injunctions on, not for reasons of security but so the Board could choose who represented the men and the men didn't have their choice. But we did eventually get the injunctions lifted. To achieve support of the Unions we had to demonstrate against the area officers, so we occupied the NUM office in Dover. The area official was Jack Collins, who was fully supportive, Comrade Collins was always supportive."

The officers of the other two branches were not supportive of the financial outlay to have the injunctions lifted.

We occupied the area office and had a campaign and eventually Tilmanstone being closed, Snowdon being closed – those officials weren't any longer with us, so we had the injunctions lifted in Court – the Coal Board capitulated legally." (John Moyle, 2006)

The last months at Betteshanger included yet another tragedy, with the last man to die in Betteshanger pit. On June 15 1989, Geoff Almond died, a father of three who was buried 'under tonnes of slurry while cleaning a conveyor belt'. He managed to shout to his colleagues to run from the danger area. The Union pointed out that there had been problems in the area where he died, with slurry dropping down, but management did nothing.

In June 1989 Dennis Skinner MP asked the following question in the House of Commons about this death and the continued victimisation of the branch officials:

"Is the minister aware that a fortnight ago Geoff Almond was killed in Betteshanger colliery when he was crushed to death? John Moyle, President of the Kent Area went to the colliery. He is a victimised miner, because British Coal refused to give him his job back. Upon trying to find out about the event, which led to that tragic death, he was ordered off the premises because he was a sacked miner. It is high time that the Secretary of State for Energy or any of his accomplices had a word with British Coal. When victimised miners who are trying to resolve and find out the cause of such tragic accidents are ordered off the premises, it shows that it is high time that British Coal and all its allies gave up this lust for revenge." (Hansard, 26th June 1989)

Management tried to change working practices to the detriment of the men. The attempts to change working practices and grind men down was noted by everybody:

"They wanted 24 hour working, 7 days a week, so they came at the lads and the lads was in a weak position, un-organized. The came at us like bulls at a red rag. They started with the discipline and sending people out, restriction of wages and allowances, redeployment, downgrading.Where you'd have protection of earnings of £7/8 a day, if that work wasn't available; they'd transfer you to a lower rate. The pressures was starting to come on. Training was a thing of the past; the mining college at Canterbury was run down. One of the things was the shift pattern, which we fought them on, they wanted 7 days a week, 24 hours a day production and they wanted to smash our traditional holidays, which was 3 weeks a year, last week in July, first two weeks in August." (John Moyle, 2006)

It was hard for the union to organise:

"We had good Chargemen (Pufflers), what in most industries you'd call Shop Stewards, they ran each district, so mainly you had to win them; men are not sheep, but I also think there was loyalty to me and the others as sacked miners. We controlled it; we controlled production from outside the pit, in that office down the road (Magness House) 2½ miles from the pit. But all the time these campaigns were taking place outside the pit, we couldn't speak to the men, we couldn't even get in the pit canteen. We tried to buy land to build a new Union office, to put a Portacabin outside the pit. We couldn't get Planning Permission from the local Council; we couldn't even get permission from the Parish Council for a bit of land on the corner that we (the Miners Welfare) had given them! A couple of times I got mass meetings in a field, but they depended on the weather – in the summer time.

Industrial relations was at a horrendous low. They still had a lot of pride and principle in their hearts, they detested the bastards who was walking around with a book and timing and telling them what to do." (John Moyle, 2006)

Battle for the bonus

In 1980, miners were the highest paid in the energy industry, with an average Earning of £77 per week. Of the others, Atomic Energy paid £70, Gas £49, and Electricity supply workers earned £62.

In 1988, Electricity supply was top at £139, with Gas at £124 and Mining £120.

One of the large battles, after the national strike, surrounded a new incentive bonus scheme. On 13th September 1988, the Coal Board gave four weeks notice of terminating the old scheme. This had been a scheme where *everyone* benefited from additional bonus earnings.

Under the old scheme there was a sense of camaraderie, as the bonus system was applied to the production of the pit as a whole. A collective effort was called for. The Coal Board wanted to make bonuses payable to individuals. Thereby splitting workers up, trying to get them to compete with each other, rather than help one another.

"What we had in Kent was unique. It was based on a principle that one individual collier wouldn't have a rate of pay. But at each pit you'd have an amount of money created/earned and it was dished out among the production workers, part of that money went into an area pot for anyone on the surface, a non-production worker, on haulage, on transport and those sort of things. It didn't matter if you were running haulage in Betteshanger or Tilmanstone or Snowdon, you'd get the same bonus. It kept everyone together. They wanted to smash it; they hated it.

There was a lot of conscientiousness, people liked to produce coal. In a pit, when you are producing coal on a production unit, which is producing a lot, the actual work, most of the time, is easier than when you are not producing – you're fighting it, it breaks down, you're humping steel and conveyors and cables and supports or its rough, there's falls of ground. You're working in horrendously bad conditions, there's stone on the floor, there's a lot of dust when you are trying to cut the floor to get the height. The coal's very thin, so you're struggling, so it balanced itself up; you'd have a lot of bravado, one team would say 'you lazy f…bastard!' and the so-called lazybones would say, 'wait for the docket at the weekend, you'll see who put the £ in the pot, that's how it worked. The lads had a bit of conscientiousness, they knew each day if they was turning a dollar. So it brought the men together, so they'd all stick together.

Management wanted absolutely individual production units, they wanted individual bonus for workers at pits. We were up against that, it had come in all over the country.

Tilmanstone and Snowdon had accepted it. We was left here at Betteshanger with us outside the gates campaigning that it wasn't going to happen." (John Moyle, 2006)

However the Board hadn't given the required three months notice to end the Bonus, so the Branch took the NCB to Court for Breach of Contract and they won. The Board was compelled to give three months notice. The Branch believed that then they would stop the new bonus scheme, but the national union did not have the funds to resist the Board's action.

The Closure

Before looking into the closure of Betteshanger itself, it is necessary to briefly refer to the Thatcher Government's pit closure process. The unions were compelled to accept 'The Review Procedure' or face closure. Thatcher's closures expressed fundamental political opposition to union power and socialism as a whole. As the NUM was one of the most powerful unions of the time, if they were to fall, then trade unionism would be damaged. The workers' power would be substantially broken. Miners had after all effectively ended the career of Thatcher's predecessor, Ted Heath, only ten years earlier.

This didn't mean, however, that workers' rights were to be given up so easily. And Betteshanger still had plenty of fight left.

They had stood by Tilmanstone, who were threatened with closure in 1987.

"For far too long the NCB has waged a filthy war of attrition against Tilmanstone, with the aim to try to close the pit. They are Industrial Saboteurs." (Betteshanger Branch minutes)

A leaflet in support of the Tilmanstone miners was issued:

"The demand for Kent coal will continue to grow, due to its clean quality in combating Acid Rain.... uncertainty from South Africa and international energy policy changes after the nuclear disaster in the USSR.

Don't be drawn into co-operation and collaboration – its only reward is the dole. Miners have died, being imprisoned and are on dole to secure jobs at Tilmanstone." (Betteshanger Branch leaflet, 1987)

The Thatcher regime's 'Review Procedure' was more 'Closure Procedure' and Tilmanstone went under. They were later joined by Snowdown. The NUM were now committed to keeping the last pit in Kent open, Betteshanger.

In July 1989 movements were made to close the pit suddenly. Betteshanger did not vote for its own closure.

Different stories are told about what happened at Betteshanger in August 1989, but it is clear that neither the Branch, the men, nor the Committee voted for closure or to withdraw from the Review Procedure.

Joe Dickenson (NUM branch secretary) wrote on the 27th July to Mr. Wheeler, the Manager. He proposed reconvening the Colliery Review Meeting on the 4th September because the pit was to be shut from 31st July for holidays.

But management took the arrival of the summer holidays in July 1989, when many people, including the Branch Chairman, were away, to push for a decision to accept redundancy quickly. Mr Wheeler claimed that the redundancy offer had to be agreed by the 26th August and a notice was posted at pit to that effect.

> "They said people had to accept the offer very quickly or the redundancy terms would be withdrawn. This bribed a number of people to sign." (Terry Harrison, 2006)

The local paper reported that:

> "By offering the redundancy terms only until August 26, after which the sums on offer plummet, they are scaring people into applying (for it). People were signing on in case the pit closed and thus British Coal could say there was no will to continue." (East Kent Mercury, August 24th 1989).

The maximum sums on offer compared with State Redundancy were huge:

	Board Offer	State pension
37 years old	£21,288	£2,788
47 years old	£29,772	£3,772
57 years old	£38,090	£4,592

It was reported to the Branch, on 25th August 1989, that Terry Harrison had said:

"If we can get men to withdraw their notices, we might have a chance. The Committee then went to the Colliery and spoke to about 100-150 men in Betts Club, spelling out the situation, by this time nearly all the men had signed." (NUM Branch minutes, August 1989)

In the files there are copies of two letters sent on subsequent days in August to the National NUM. One asking to stay in the Review Procedure and one asking to withdraw from it, that is to accept closure. The carbon copies of the letters show that Joe Dickenson, Branch Secretary at the time, *did not sign* the latter or any letter asking to withdraw from the Procedure and therefore close the pit.

As is clear on the carbon copy, the letter requesting closure was originally shown to be signed by Wes Chambers with his title, The National Delegate. This title is then typed over with the words Branch Secretary; suggesting Joe Dickenson had signed it. But Joe Dickenson was not aware of the contents of this letter.

There was also, at the time, some distress at the role of the National Union officers in the closure. Later they did not take out an injunction against salvage operations, which prevented the pit continuing as a co-operative in the future.

"I was on salvage for 3 months when they brought the pithead down on 26 November. I'd been hanging on a rope under the headgear for 30 years, to see it come down, that landmark, it was so sad. To see the landmark since 1924 decimated, cut through like a liquorice, as if it was nothing, it was terrible to see." (Coalfield Heritage Initiative Kent CHIK, Respondent, Dover Museum, 2007)

"I never expected to have to look for another job. On that last day I was on the pit yard, waiting to prepare for salvage on 28s coalface. This team just gave up; they were coming down to get their wage packet and they shouted across to the lamp room 'we've had enough, we've had a gut full; we're not coming, not one man turned up for work." (Second CHIK Respondent, Dover Museum, 2007)

The pithead finally came down in November 1989.

Once the pit was closed, you might think that the battle for Betteshanger was over. Not a bit of it, the fighting spirit lived on. The struggle continued on many fronts: The last attempt to continue coaling; the building of a co-op for sacked miners; the battle for justice for the victimised; the fight for compensation claims and the continuation of the Miner's Welfare.

The NUM Kent Area was wound up by the National Union by the end of 1989, although the sacked men remained members for life of the National Union of Mineworkers. The officers of the Betteshanger Branch continued to support all the outstanding business of its local members.

The last minute of the last active meeting of Betteshanger NUM branch read:

"Any other business.
Must record J Moyle's effort for his work for this Branch (and the community) and the meeting congratulated him, and thanked him wholeheartedly." (J Young, End of 1989)

The attempt to form a Mining Workers Co-operative

The Board moved rapidly to try to remove every physical memory of the existence of Betteshanger. Their first efforts were to remove machinery and equipment, worth tens of thousands of pounds, from the pit, by way of salvage. The Branch decided to stop the salvage because it was conducting serious negotiations to buy the pit and run it as a Worker's Co-op.

The Branch minutes report:

Salvage operations

"We must keep going, in the hope we keep the shafts open. Big businesses are now looking at the Pit."

Campaign on the Pit, regarding salvage been curtailed with injunctions on us. Took advisors on and held a Press Conference in London. Knowing that the Board were meeting. The Coal Board on Thursday said Betts wouldn't be discussed, but on Friday the Board did discuss it, and it went to the vote, and we lost it only by one vote, so if we had been able to curtail the salvage operations, we had been in with a good chance of Betteshanger re-opening."
(NUM Minutes, 1989)

This attempt to buy Betteshanger and run it as a Worker's Co-operative mining coal was on roughly the same basis as the existing Tower Colliery in South Wales. But this was defeated, in Kent; the NCB would not allow it to happen at Betteshanger.

After this further defeat, attention was turned to finding employment for the sacked and victimised. We have already described how the sacked men were not able to find employment. Years later, some found work as Care Assistants, School Caretakers or in casual work as a long distance lorry drivers. But victimised miners were refused work digging the channel tunnel and even marched off that site when they had obtained work through an agency. Even Councillor Terry Birkett, then leader of

Dover District Council, who had visited the channel tunnel workings in his official capacity, was refused a job on the tunnel.

The sacked men met with victimisation from all directions. The Social Welfare Scheme minutes from September 1984 read:

> "Freshwater fishing members were being prevented from going to the fishing pond by the Police – because they were sacked miners."

The victimised did not sit down and accept the situation they faced. As distinct from the Mining Workers Co-operative, they set up a Building Co-operative to find work.

The Building Co-operative

The NUM Branch Minutes report:

> "Co-operative formed now, by members, no individuals own it, firstly to get the victimised men established, and then any members who wish to join it."

When the National/Area NUM left their Dover office, the Kent union was now run from the Betteshanger premises at Magness house. There was now only one NUM Branch in the whole of Kent. The National union gave the remaining branch £29,000, from the area funds, the rest of which reverted to the National. The Branch chairman asked for permission to use some of this money for the co-operative, but the National said they must not spend a penny of it. The Branch however donated £4,000 for the co-operative out of its general fund.

The Betteshanger Building Co-operative (BECOL) lasted 3 years, winning contracts from Dover District Council for external painting and decoration of its Council Houses.

The purpose of the co-op was to enable the sacked men to have a new last employer, other than the Coal Board, who could give them references.

In order to have someone to write the references, so the men would no longer be blacklisted and denied work, the structure was formally that of a company with a Managing Director. Once this had been achieved and men had new jobs BECOL was closed.

BECOL Van

Betteshanger Social Welfare Scheme and the Coalfield Industrial Social Welfare Organisation (CISWO)

Since 1989, the interests of miners continued to be served from Magness House via the Betteshanger Social Welfare Scheme charity BSWS (part of CISWO).

This is a charitable organisation. It is jointly run by two groups, the Coalfield Industrial Social Welfare Organisation, supported by, and on behalf of, the NUM, and, secondly, the Coal Board. But during the strike, and thereafter, the Coal Board withdrew its Trustees from the Charity. Kent was the only area not to have CISWO meetings during the dispute.

At the same time the Betteshanger Social Welfare Scheme was in financial difficulty. Only the National Association of Colliery Overmen and Deputies (NACODS) were paying funds into it.

The minutes of the Charity recognised that the Betteshanger Social Clubs:

" ...had been at the backbone of the scheme, over the last 12 months it has been a good ally to the community in feeding the village and raising funds." (Social Welfare Scheme minutes, 1985)

On the eve of the strike the charity had only £400 in its accounts (Branch minutes, 30th December 1983). Now in 2007, due to substantial physical and financial support from the Betteshanger Branch NUM, it has considerable capital assets, including a large sports and social club in Mill Hill, Deal. Its priority project is to start providing purpose built accommodation for retired and disabled miners and widows.

After the strike, the charity continued its activities on behalf of the miners and their descendants by operating the Mine Worker's Compensation Scheme. This national compensation scheme was to recompense miners, and their widows and descendants, for the terrible injuries they suffered in mining coal. These varied from deafness, through industrial noise, to accidents, or loss of fingers or limbs. But the majority of cases concerned Vibro-White Finger and bronchitis/emphysema. As someone described to me not every miner who ingested coal and stone dust contracted bronchitis/emphysema, but every miner who worked underground next to the compression drills and jigger picks was deafened.

Vibro-White Finger is a condition that affects the arms, hands, wrists, fingers or thumbs. It is related to, or contributed to, by exposure to vibration. Symptoms include blanching or numbness of the fingers and pins and needles. It can also lead to reduced dexterity of the fingers and hand.

Industrial disease and accident killed many miners. The minute books at Betteshanger NUM constantly contain the refrain:

"The meeting commenced with members standing in respect for (so and so) who had died".

Miners and ex-minors die young, or live out their years with the pain of injury and wheezing chests.

In various parts of the country, and parts of Kent, some miners went through compensation solicitors who charged the individual miners a hefty percentage, up to 10% sometimes, out of their own compensation. In other parts of the country the Union of Democratic Miners (UDM) participated in this scam, as reported in the media in spring 2007.

At Betteshanger, the situation was different. The Social Welfare Scheme (BSWS) did not levy such a percentage. All cases were passed through one reputable solicitor, O H Parsons, who was properly, separately paid and not from the individual miner's compensation. In return, individual miners or their families were asked to donate a mere 3% of the damages to the NUM, now the Welfare Scheme, up to a maximum of £150. There were cases at Betteshanger where the individual's compensation rightly reached five figures and BSWS only took £150. The record book for the compensation has thirty full pages of records, with thirty-nine entries a page and one with thirteen.

This covers at least 1170 compensation cases taken since the pit closed. Betteshanger employed only 2,000 men at one time, but the cases go back over a number of generations and years. This shows the extent of the injury and damage to miner's bodies, health and lives. The charity has also acted in the interests of ex-mineworkers, their widows and descendants.

As well as providing this service the charity originally ran two social clubs. One in Betteshanger village and the other in Cowdray Square.

In 1996, the old Cowdray Square Miners' Welfare Club took UDI from BSWS, became independent and set up separately.

In 1999, the charity won grants to build a new social and sports club, at a cost of £1.4M. The grants received totalled £1,026,994 including £849,497 from English Sports Council (Lottery Grant). The balance was raised by BSWS and its members.

SIXTY YEARS OF STRUGGLE

As a local newspaper reported:

> "Ten years ago when Betteshanger closed, people thought we would not continue. But we have lived from hand to mouth and week to week on donations from miners and the community. In 5-10 years the Club will probably be debt free. People were elated, especially when British Coal walked away, leaving us with nothing. Local people will see that there is still life after industry turned its back. Activities include: bowls, cricket, rugby, football, brass band, allotments, freshwater fishing, and garden club." (1999)

The Club also provides a venue for social events, with a bar and facilities for bowls, darts, cricket and brass band practice.

In Betteshanger village, the second club, until recently the old Welfare Club, has looked just as it has for many years, certainly since I first visited it in 1972. It too is run by sacked miners.

But in the 21st Century moves started to refurbish the Betteshanger village club and create a community centre. Attempts were then made to set up a rival independent, privately owned club, which would not retain the heritage and links with the coal industry. This independent club was supported by the local MP, Parish Council and The South East England Development Agency. Capital money and land was offered from public funds to this private company. Once the village turned against this idea, with a petition signed by the people, then monies to upgrade and refurbish the old club instead to a community centre were not forthcoming, twice being refused support from the Coalfields Regeneration Trust.

The battle for the village club and heritage of Betteshanger continues with attempts to obtain funding for improvements from other organisations and individuals. This continues with the support of Betteshanger Social Welfare Scheme.

In some ways the divisions of the strike live on in the attempt to remove the Betteshanger village club from its heritage. Built by donations from miners, run largely by sacked miners its continued existence as part of the Miners Social Welfare Scheme is a way of holding on to the important heritage of miners working and dying in the service of coal.

On the site of the Pit, by which the club still stands, apart from the Miners' 'walking trail', there is no mark of the heritage. No record of the 60 years of industrial struggle. There is no monument for the miners and their families who tramped down from the North, from Wales and Scotland. Nothing for the miners' victimised after the 1926 and 1984 strikes. No record of the miners who stood up against the bullying of boys in the 1930s. No testament to those who occupied the pit to save jobs in 1960 and 1984 or their a leading role in the National Strikes. And there is no visible testimony to the work of the Kent Women Against Pit Closures.

This book is a tribute to those miners and their families, to the mining community of Betteshanger. It is a tribute to class struggle, to workers standing together to defend their interests and fighting for jobs and justice. Battles almost forgotten today.

Just as miners worked in the dark, carrying a small light, so this book aims to be a light in the dark, of different times, a light of celebration, hope and example.

It is written to express my deepest respect to all these men and women. To the heroes who have struggled for sixty years and prevailed. It has been a privilege to record your history.

There will come a time when these strong, heroic struggles are valued again.

Di Parkin 2007

SIXTY YEARS OF STRUGGLE

GLOSSARY

Agent	Regional area secretary of the union.
Air Doors	Airtight, wooden framed doors.
Belt	Conveyor.
Butty System	System where one man took on and paid miners.
Cage	The lift that took men down and coal up.
Colliers	Men who got coal from the face.
Contract Man	Someone working in a team who was contracted at a certain rate.
Deputy & Overman	Front line supervisor.
Docket	Wage slip for whole team.
Double chucking	Throwing the coal over the new track onto the conveyor, before moving the pans over.
Dust-money	Financial allowance for working in dust.
Essential Work Orders	Name for payments that were made to men who were not able to do their normal work.
Fifth columnist	Derogatory term for a traitor.
Floor Blowing	Where the bottom of the coal seam was rising up making it hard to work.
Gate	One end of the coalface.

Jig	Steep incline gate used as a gravity haulage system; full tubs going down pulling empty tubs up.
Jigger pick	Mechanical pick using compressed air.
Lamp	Cap lamp without which miners could not go down the Pit. They left a tally on their hook to show they were down. (see Tally)
Market Man	Someone who didn't have a regular job, but was sent to fill in.
Monkey Puffler	Puffler's Assistant elected by teams. (see Puffler)
National Association for Freedom.	
	Right wing pressure group.
National Power Loading Agreement	
	Change to the wage payment system, meaning no contracts, every face worker paid the same.
Nystagma	Blindness from working in coal dust.
Pans	Where the coal is loaded onto the conveyor.
Pan-turners/Pan-men	
	Men who moved the belts and conveyors over, so coal could be taken away from the face
Pneumoconiosis	Disease of the lungs caused by an accumulation of dust, especially from coal, asbestos, or silica
Puffler	Representative of the men elected by teams on the coalface.

Rag up	Wild cat strike.
Relief payments	Welfare payments.
Riding the pit	Coming out of the pit.
Rippers	Men who set the steel rings to advance the headings and roadways of the face.
Shaftsman/Winder	NUM member who "wound" the cages down and up the pit shaft.
Sequestrators	Government appointed who took away the NUM funds in 1984 strike.
Silicosis	An occupational lung disease that develops over time when dust that contains silica is inhaled into the lungs.
Snap	Food taken down the pit.
20s	Name of coal face, also '4s'. Etc.
Stint	Area of coal to be taken off by each collier
Tally	Tag left on hook in lamp room to show lamp had been taken and man was down the pit.
Water-money	Allowance for working in water.
Winding house	Pithead where the cages were wound down and up.
Waiting time	Time spent unproductively waiting for materials.

ACKNOWLEDGEMENTS

This book could never have been written without the assistance of these people, especially the miners, their families and others who remembered their lives. My thanks and greatest respect to:

> Wilf Aldred, Dennis Bent, Terry Birkett, Josephine Dempster (for transcribing the records of her father Albert Newton), Joe Dickenson, Janet Dunn, Paul Dunn, Lesley Fowler, Mary Fowler, Liz French, Terry Harrison, Peter Holden, Mr & Mrs Grant, John Macgahie, John Moyle, Kate Moyle, Dickie Prescott, Arthur Scargill, Sheila Shooter, John Thirkell, Dickie Tank, Sylvia Watson, Albert Welford, Cynthia White, Mrs. Wells, Mrs. Williams.

> Also for their advice and assistance, Simon Exton, Keith Flett and the London Socialist Historians, Andrew Glyn, Hilda Kean, Dave Lyddon, Lynda Pearse, John Tosh, Paul Thompson,

> Sarah Snell for typing the script and Andrew Williams for editing and designing the book.

The archives at Mass Observation at the University of Sussex and CHIK in the Dover Museum together with the Kent Archivists at Whitfield and Maidstone.

Kent County Council and the National Lottery for the grants.

All photographs provided by CHIK at Dover Museum

Above all, the Trustees of the Betteshanger Social Welfare Scheme have been a wonderful source of support and encouragement.

Thanks to all who have contributed to the creation of this history. However, any errors or oversights are mine and mine alone.

Di Parkin November 2007

BIBLIOGRAPHY

Allen, V L	The Militancy of British Miners. The Moor Press 1981
Arnot, R P	The Miners: A History of the Miners' Federation of Great Britain. Allen & Unwin 1949
Beynon, Huw	Digging Deeper: Issues in the Miner's Strike. London: Verso 1985
Coulter, J A	A State of Siege. Politics and Policing of the Coalfields: Miners' Strike 1984. J Couler, S Miller and M Walker. Canary Press 1984
Douglass, D A	A Miners' Life: D Douglas, J Kreiger. Routledge & Kegan Paul, 1983
Early, Tommy	Miners' strike 1984-85: Poems by Tommy Early. NUM Kent 1985
Glynn, A and Machin, S	The Labour Market: Consequences of Technical and Structural Change. Discussion paper series. No 7. Colliery Closure and the Decline of the UK Coal Industry. October 1996
Goffee, Robert	Kent Miners: Stability and Change in Work and Community 1927-1976. PHD 1978: University of Kent. The Butty System and the Kent Coalfield. Bulletin of the Society for the Study of Labour History 1977, 34 pp
Harkell, G	The Migration of Mining Families to the Kent coalfield between the wars. Oral History 1978, 6.1 pp 92-113

Harrison, N   Once a Miner. U.O.P, 1954 (reprinted by CHIK)

Dennis Henriques   Coal is our Life. 1956
and Slaughter

Johnson, W   The Development of the Kent Coalfield 1896
                         – 1946. PhD Kent 1972

Kneif, Mary Ann   Directed to the Mines; the Bevin Boys, 1943-1948
                         PhD. Kent 2005

Llewellyn, Ross   Hersden, Chisley Colliery Village. Private
                         Publication. 2003

D Parkin   PhD thesis: Nation, Class and Gender in Second
                         World War Britain. LSE. 1987

Pitt, M   The World on Our Backs. The Kent Miners and
                         the 1972 Miners' Strike. London. Lawrence and
                         Wishard 1979

Rutherford, Barbara   The Coming of the Miners. Deal Society
                         Magazine Vol 1 #18 Summer 1976

Samuel, R   The Enemy Within: Pit Villages and the
                         Miners' strike of 1984/5. Edited by R Samuel, b
                         Bloomfield. G Boanas. Routledge & Kegan Paul
                         1986.

Taylor, Warwick   The Forgotten Conscript: A History of the Bevan
                         Boys. Pentland Press 1995

132

Branden
Bell

This book tells the story of Betteshanger colliery's proud history, standing up for workers' rights from 1926 to 1989.

With interviews with people who were there from the beginning, the sinkers, and those who desperately tramped there from across the UK in the 1930s. It has tales of all the major disputes: strikes over bullying in the 1930s, the illegal war time strike in 1942, the stay down strikes of 1960 & 1984, and the key role Betteshanger played in the national strikes of 1972, 1974 and 1984.

Di Parkin first met Betteshanger miners on a picket line in 1972, then in the 1984 strike and again at the twentieth anniversary of that strike.

She wrote about the 1942 dispute in her PHD, before reuniting with Betteshanger miners in 2004 to create this dramatic history of their struggle.

✦

This book is produced thanks to the Trustees of the Betteshanger Social Welfare Scheme and grants from National Lottery Awards for all and Kent County Council.

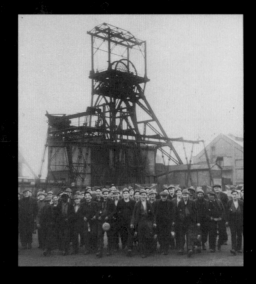

ISBN 978-0-9557550-0-2

9 780955 755002 >

Price £4.99